EYEWITNESS TRAVEL

TOP 10
CYPRUS

JACK HUGHES

Top 10 Cyprus Highlights

The Top 10 of Everything

CONTENTS

Cyprus Area by Area

Streetsmart

Within each Top 10 list in this book, no hierarchy of quality or popularity is implied. All 10 are, in the editor's opinion, of roughly equal merit.

Front cover and spine *A pirate ship seen through a natural arch in Cape Gkreko, Ayia Napa*
Back cover *A traditional street in Ayia Napa*
Title page *Fishing boats moored at the harbour in Kyrenia*

The information in this DK Eyewitness Top 10 Travel Guide is checked regularly. Every effort has been made to ensure that this book is as up-to-date as possible at the time of going to press. Some details, however, such as telephone numbers, opening hours, prices, gallery hanging arrangements and travel information, are liable to change. The publishers cannot accept responsibility for any consequences arising from the use of this book, nor for any material on third party websites, and cannot guarantee that any website address in this book will be a suitable source of travel information. We value the views and suggestions of our readers very highly. Please write to: Publisher, DK Eyewitness Travel Guides, Dorling Kindersley, 80 Strand, London WC2R 0RL, Great Britain, or email travelguides@dk.com

Welcome to
Cyprus

Cyprus is an island that will challenge you with its complex political history, dazzle you with its breathtaking landscapes and beaches, and delight you with the hospitality of its people. It is a Mediterranean holiday destination that is, quite simply, like no other. With Eyewitness Top 10 Cyprus, it's yours to explore.

The long history of Cyprus is visible in the physical landscape. You can walk in the footsteps of Mycenaeans and Romans at **Kourion**, **Kato Pafos** and **Amathous**; explore stone-age settlements on the **Akamas Peninsula**; and discover treasures of Byzantine religious art in the churches of the **Troödos Mountains**.

More recent history is reflected in **Nicosia**, the world's last divided capital city. It is a unique experience to cross its border, observing how the smart shopping street of Ledra transforms into a Turkish-style medina, dominated by its magnificent **Selimiye Mosque**.

The island also boasts glorious beaches and year-round sun. If you're based at any of the main resorts you'll find family-friendly activities and superb water sports, along with bars, restaurants and cafés, and an often hedonistic nightlife, of which lively **Ayia Napa** is the party capital.

Whether you are here for a few days or several weeks, our Top 10 guide is designed to bring together the best of everything Cyprus has to offer. It gives you tips throughout, from seeking out what's free to finding the best restaurants, along with five easy-to-follow itineraries, which cover a clutch of sights in a short space of time. Add inspiring photography and detailed maps, and you've got the essential pocket-sized travel companion. **Enjoy the book, and enjoy Cyprus**.

Clockwise from top: **Cape Gkreko, Ayia Napa; the rooftops of Nicosia; Saranda Kolones, Kato Pafos Archaeological Park; Roman Odeon, Kourion; fresco at Agios Neofytos Monastery; Agioi Anargyroi church at Cape Gkreko, Ayia Napa; Cypriots sit outside at Arsos**

Exploring Cyprus

Whether your visit is short or long, these itineraries will ensure that you experience the very best Cyprus has to offer. They cover all the island's archaeological and historic highlights, the best of

its spectacular beaches, its top beauty spots and some of the most atmospheric and lively towns.

The Troödos range is famous for its Byzantine churches.

Two Days in Cyprus

Day ❶
MORNING
Make an early start in **Larnaka** *(see p78)*, allowing time to explore the **Pierides Foundation**'s eclectic exhibits *(see pp18–19)*. Stroll to the harbour for lunch, then head to **Nicosia** *(see pp12–13)*.
AFTERNOON
Explore this astonishing walled city, taking in the historical sights, the **Cyprus Museum** *(see pp14–15)* and shops. Cross the border into **North Nicosia** *(see p109)*, shopping for handicrafts at the Ottoman **Büyük Han** *(see p13)*.

Day ❷
MORNING
Head into the **Troödos Mountains** *(see p102)* to visit the extraordinary painted churches *(see pp28–9)*. Enjoy a pine-forest stroll, then drive to **Pafos** *(see pp92–3)* on the coast.
AFTERNOON
After a seafood lunch, visit **Kato Pafos Archaeological Park** *(see pp30–31)*. End the day in historic **Limassol** *(see pp24–5)*, travelling there via the ruins of **Amathous** *(see pp20–21)*.

Lakki Polis
Kathikas
Coral Bay
Lempa
Neolithic Village
Pafos
Kato Pafos
Archaeological
Park
Troödos Mountains
Omodos
Ancient
Amathou
Kourion
Limassol

0 kilometres   20
0 miles   20

Seven Days in Cyprus

Day ❶
Start your explorations in **Nicosia** *(see pp12–13)*. Shop for souvenirs in **Laiki Geitonia**, pay a visit to the **Cyprus Museum** *(see pp14–15)* and step into the **AG Leventis Gallery** *(see p38)* to contemplate the fine collection of European and modern Cypriot art. Enjoy a leisurely lunch in the courtyard of the traditional **Boghjalian Konak Restaurant** *(see p115)*, and then spend the rest of the day perusing the shops and exploring the old town.

Amathous is a fascinating ancient site.

Key
— Two-day itinerary
— Seven-day itinerary

○ Kyrenia

② Nicosia

Agia Napa ○

Larnaka ○

(see p85), with its pet pelican. Later, get ready for a night on the town. Start your evening with a drink in **Plateia Seferi** *(see p16)*, the main square, before heading off to enjoy some of the best nightlife on the island.

Day ④

Head down the coast to **Larnaka** *(see p78)* and visit the **Pierides Foundation** *(see pp18–19)*, then continue on to **Limassol** *(see pp24–5)*. On your way, stop off to explore the ruins of ancient **Amathous** *(see pp20–21)*.

Day ⑤

Travel west out of Limassol to the ancient site of **Kourion** *(see pp26–7)*, and then inland to the **Troödos Mountains** *(see p102)*. Marvel at the Byzantine churches *(see pp28–9)* before enjoying lunch in a traditional tavern. Finish up at **Omodos** *(see p106)*, where you can visit the town's magnificent monastery, browse the shops and enjoy a taste of the local wine.

Day ⑥

Head for Pafos and the spellbinding **Kato Pafos Archaeological Park** *(see pp30–31)*. You can easily spend several hours exploring the site before enjoying a seafood lunch overlooking the waves. Afterwards, bask on the beach or take one of the boat rides from the harbour, before exploring the shops. Visit the nearby wine village of **Kathikas** for dinner on the terrace of **Yiannis Taverna** *(see p99)*.

Day ②

Cross into **North Nicosia** *(see p109)* on Ledra Street and take in the highlights, including the **Selimiye Mosque** *(see p12)* and **Büyük Han** *(see p13)*. Wander around the market and pick up some spices and sweet treats. Grab a quick bite at one of the kebab stands, and then begin making your way to **Kyrenia** *(see p109)*. Explore this picturesque harbour and enjoy a seafood dinner overlooking the waves.

Cyprus Museum artifact

Day ③

Return to **Nicosia** and then head to **Ayia Napa** *(see pp16–17)* for a leisurely swim and lunch at **Vassos**

Day ⑦

Travel to the unspoiled **Akamas Peninsula** *(see pp32–3)*, making your first stop at **Lempa Neolithic Village** *(see p94)*, followed by some relaxing beach time at tranquil **Coral Bay** *(see p95)*. Continue to **Polis** *(see p94)*, for a stroll around this picturesque small village, followed by a catch-of-the-day fresh seafood dinner at one of the superb restaurants lining the small harbour at **Lakki** *(see p33)*.

Top 10 Cyprus Highlights

Ruins of ancient Kourion

Cyprus Highlights

Cyprus packs a remarkable set of attractions into a small space: museums and archaeological sites spanning over five millennia, lively beach resorts, and a landscape of forests, vineyards and olive groves. As an island where you can swim and ski all in the same day, this holiday paradise has something for everyone.

① Nicosia Walled City

This divided city, set within medieval ramparts, is full of interest. With a clutch of excellent museums, historic buildings, a lively market and authentic cafés and restaurants, it merits a leisurely visit (see pp12–13).

② Cyprus Museum, Nicosia

This superb museum displays a range of finds from Stone Age to Roman sites all over the island. Highlights include ancient sculptures and a collection of thousands of terracotta figurines (see pp14–15).

③ Ayia Napa

This resort is the liveliest spot in Cyprus, with great beaches, water sports and a huge number of bars, cafés and restaurants to suit every taste (see pp16–17).

Pierides Museum, Larnaka ④

Founded by a 19th-century philanthropist keen to rescue Cyprus's vanishing heritage, this collection extends from the Neolithic era to the medieval period (see pp18–19).

5 Ancient Amathous

It takes a little imagination to picture Amathous in ancient times based on the fragments of walls that still remain, but this hillside site is proof of the city's glorious past *(see pp20–21)*.

6 Historic Limassol

Narrow market streets full of food stalls and craft workshops surround the sturdy medieval castle in the heart of the old quarter. Mosques and minarets are reminders of the island's multicultural history *(see pp24–5)*.

7 Kourion

The multi-tiered stone theatre here is the summer setting for concerts, and offers fine views over the peninsula *(see pp26–7)*.

8 Troödos Painted Churches

The stone walls of these old Orthodox sanctuaries, hidden away in the Troödos mountains, conceal a unique treasury of vividly coloured frescoes depicting scenes from the Old and New Testaments *(see pp28–9)*.

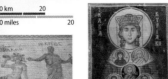

9 Kato Pafos Archaeological Park

The superb mosaics that adorned the floors of lavish villas built at Pafos in its Roman Imperial heyday are now part of a UNESCO World Heritage Site. Today they are one of the island's top historical attractions *(see pp30–31)*.

10 Akamas Peninsula

The hillsides and headlands of the Akamas form the island's last undeveloped frontier. Here, on Cyprus's only uncrowded beaches, turtles come each year to nest *(see pp32–3)*.

🔟 ⭐ Nicosia Walled City

Modern Nicosia is a cheerfully rambling sprawl that surrounds a picturesque inner core ringed by impressive fortifications. Unlike many historic town centres, this carefully preserved medieval gem is still very much a living town, its streets bustling with shops, lively bars and restaurants. Pockets of restored buildings, such as the Archbishop's Palace and museums, reveal a glorious Byzantine past. The city is famously divided and it is a fascinating experience to visit both sides of the border. The northern part reflects a vibrant Turkish culture, while the south remains resoundingly Greek.

1 Medieval Walls
Five of the 11 bastions **(above)** strengthening the ramparts are in the southern part of Nicosia.

2 Pafos Gate
This gate is only 10 m (30 ft) from the Turkish zone. Inside, the Church of the Holy Cross straddles the border and its rear door, in the north zone, is always sealed.

3 Selimiye Mosque
This mosque **(below)** can be seen from both sides of the border. It was built during the 13th century as a French Gothic church, and became a mosque in the late 16th century.

4 Ledra Observatory
For a panoramic view of the city **(above)**, head for this observatory and small museum located on the 11th floor of the Shacolas Tower.

5 Archangelos Michael Trypiotis
Built by Archbishop Germanos II in 1695, this church is a well preserved example of the Franco-Byzantine style.

HISTORY OF NICOSIA

The site on which Nicosia stands was a settlement by the 3rd century BC. It was later occupied by the Romans, Byzantines and the Knights Templar. As capital of the Lusignan dynasty *(see p36)* it was one of the richest cities in Christendom. After the Ottoman conquest of 1570, its importance declined. In 1974 it was divided between north and south.

Map of the Walled City

6 House of Hadjigeorgakis Kornesios

The former home of the dragoman (mediator between Greeks and Turks) has been carefully renovated with 18th-century style decor **(above)**.

9 Büyük Han

This former Ottoman inn is today a charming and atmospheric space featuring craft shops set around a central courtyard.

10 Archbishop's Palace

Built in 1960, the "new" Archbishop's Palace mimics the Byzantine style of its predecessor. It is now home to the Byzantine Museum.

7 Famagusta Gate

The 16th-century Famagusta Gate has been restored and now houses the city's Municipal Cultural Centre, with a changing schedule of exhibitions.

8 Laïki Geitonia

This section of the walled city is pedestrianized and filled with cafés and craft shops **(right)**. It makes a pleasant place to pause during a tour of the rest of the old town.

NEED TO KNOW

Tourist Office: MAP P3
■ Aristokyprou 11
■ 22 674 264

Ledra Observatory: MAP P2 ■ Shacolas Tower.

Open Jun–Aug: 10am–8pm daily; Nov–Mar: 9:30am–5pm daily; Apr–May, Sep–Oct: 10am–6pm daily.

Adm: €0.85

Archangelos Michael Trypiotis: MAP P3
■ Solonos 47–9.

Open 9am–5pm daily.

House of Hadjigeorgakis Kornesios: MAP Q3
■ Patriarchou Grigoriou 20.

Open 8:30am–3:30pm Tue–Fri, 9:30am–4:30pm Sat.

Adm: €2.50

Selimiye Mosque: MAP P2

Archbishop's Palace: MAP Q2

■ Nicosia's historic walled city is compact and it is easy to explore the main sights on foot. If you arrive by car, leave your vehicle at the Tripoli Bastion car park (located just south of the Pafos Gate).

TOP 10 ★ Cyprus Museum, Nicosia

The Cyprus Museum is world-class in every way. A treasury of ancient finds, ranging from the earliest Stone Age and Bronze Age civilizations through to the remnants of the Late Roman Empire, it is laid out in a way that brings the island's unique heritage back to life. Set in a historic 19th-century building, the museum also benefits from its compact size and lack of crowds. Everything here is worth seeing, but don't miss the wonderful collection of ancient terracotta warriors and charioteers – some the size of toy soldiers, others as large as life.

1 Neolithic Artifacts
Early Cypriots were Neolithic tool-makers, and their flint blades and implements are on display as you enter the museum. The collection also includes Chalkolithic picrolite figurines.

2 Terracotta Warriors
This amazing army of terracotta votive figurines **(above)** was discovered at the shrine at Agia Irini, dating from the 7th and 6th centuries BC. More than 2,000 statuettes were found at the site.

3 Mycenaean Bronze and Pottery
Ceramics and wine bowls made by Mycenaean settlers are the main exhibits here, but the most striking item is a gold-inlaid bowl discovered at Enkomi.

4 Statue of Zeus
Poised to hurl a thunderbolt, a marble statue of Zeus **(left)** dominates Room 5. There are also Classical and Roman statues, including a figure of Aphrodite and three lions guarding the tombs at Tamassos.

5 Royal Tombs
Ivory carvings of mythological beasts **(above)** once adorned one of the two thrones on display in Room 11's collection of artifacts taken from the Royal Tombs at Salamis.

Floorplan of Cyprus Museum

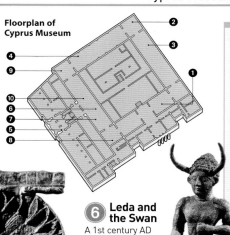

TOMB RAIDERS

Tomb raiders have plundered the island's archaeological sites for centuries. The British Museum in London and the Metropolitan Museum in New York acquired some of the Lambousa treasures legitimately, but several finds from Enkomi were sadly stolen to be sold on to antiques dealers in Europe and the rest of the world, and many other finds have vanished without trace.

6 Leda and the Swan

A 1st century AD Roman mosaic, made from red, ochre, black and white *tesserae* (tiles), depicts the myth of Leda and the Swan. It was found in the Sanctuary of Aphrodite at Palea Pafos.

10 Enkomi Treasures

The enigmatic bronze "horned god" statue **(left)** together with a splendid bowl stand decorated with animal figures are some of the highlights in this room full of finds from the Enkomi site.

7 Bronze Age Furniture

Room 11 of the museum houses furniture from the royal tomb at Salamis. Dating back to the Bronze Age, the exhibits here include an ivory inlaid throne and a bed.

8 Pit and Chamber Tombs

This eerie room recreates secret stone tombs from the Neolithic to Bronze Age periods, discovered at sites all over the island.

NEED TO KNOW

MAP N2 ▪ Leoforos Mouseiou 1 ▪ 22 865 864

Open 8am–6pm Tue–Fri (to 8pm first Wed of month), 9am–4pm Sat, 10am–1pm Sun

Adm: €4.50

▪ After your visit to the museum, cross the road to the Municipal Gardens for a cool drink in the shade at the outdoor café.

▪ If you visit on a Sunday morning, you'll find a colourful outdoor market close to the museum, which is run by expatriate Filipinos and Sri Lankans.

Statue of Septimius Severus 9

The bronze figure of the 2nd century AD Roman emperor **(right)** is one of the world's most impressive ancient Roman relics.

TOP 10 ⭐ Ayia Napa

Ayia Napa has the best beaches in Cyprus and the best nightlife in the eastern Mediterranean – so it's no surprise that this lively but laid-back resort has become a hedonistic legend in its own time, with a raucous and somewhat infamous youthful clientele. Yet Ayia Napa still retains some of the flavour of a typical Cypriot fishing port to charm visitors during the day. There's plenty for families, too, and the long sandy beaches that stretch either side of the resort mean there's still room to escape the crowds.

1 Plateia Seferi
Ayia Napa's main square is the heart of the town, surrounded by trendy bars and cafés. For most visitors it's where the evening starts – and ends.

Traditional fishing boats at Ayia Napa harbour

2 Ayia Napa Monastery
This beautiful medieval monastery is surrounded by massive defensive walls. There is an eight-sided fountain in the middle of a cloistered courtyard, entered via an arched gateway **(above)**.

3 Limanaki Harbour
Working fishing boats bob on the water alongside private yachts and large day-cruise ships in Ayia Napa's old fishing harbour. It is a little enclave of pre-tourism Cyprus, on a headland between two long sandy beaches, and a peaceful respite from the town's more familar brashness.

4 WaterWorld
This award-winning fun park offers wild, wet thrills for all ages, with various pools, water slides and roller-coaster rides. There's a shallow pool for toddlers, as well as two restaurants, a bar and a gift shop (see p59).

5 Nissi Beach
About 2 km (1.5 miles) west of town, this lovely long stretch of white sand **(above)** is one of the island's busiest and liveliest beaches in high season.

Map of Ayia Napa district

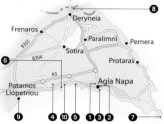

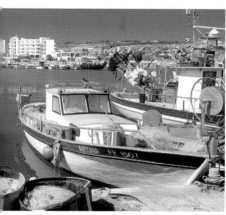

⑩ Makronissos Beach

Makronissos, also known as Golden Sands, is a long sandy stretch 1 km (half a mile) west of Nissi (and linked to it by a walkway and cycle path). It has a sweep of fine sand and plenty of water sports options.

⑥ Makronissos Tombs

Just inland from the Makronissos Beach, the Makronissos Tombs are funeral chambers that were cut into the rock during the time of Roman occupation.

⑦ Cape Gkreko

This headland (below) is the south-eastern tip of Cyprus. The view is a little spoilt by radio masts, but the clear water offers some of the best snorkelling in the area.

⑧ Varosia Gulf Viewpoint

In the village of Deryneia, 3 km (2 miles) north of Ayia Napa centre, you can look across the "Green Line" to the ghost town of Varosia, a deserted no-man's-land ever since the Turkish occupation of 1974.

⑨ Potamos Liopetriou

About 3 km (2 miles) west of Makronissos is this little fishing port and beach overlooked by a medieval watchtower.

NEED TO KNOW
MAP J4

Ayia Napa Monastery: Plateia Seferi. Open: daily

WaterWorld: Agia Thekla 18; 23 724 444; www. waterworldwaterpark. com. Open: timings vary (check the website before visiting). Adm

Makronissos Tombs: Open: daily

Varosia Gulf Viewpoint: Kennedy, Protaras; 23 741 254. Open: summer: 9:30am–7:30pm daily; winter: 9:30am–4pm daily (winter)

■ The best way to explore Ayia Napa's beaches is to rent a scooter, motorbike or bicycle – but obey basic safety rules, such as wearing a helmet. They can be hired from the many travel agencies and tour offices around the resort, or from hotels.

TOP 10 ⭐ Pierides Museum, Larnaka

This eclectic collection, which spans the ancient history of the island from prehistoric times through the Roman and Byzantine empires to the Middle Ages, is the oldest private museum in Cyprus and is still run by the Pierides family who established it in the 19th century. The displays of local crafts and costumes are among the best on the island. The museum has six rooms, together with exhibits in the entrance hall and corridors.

1 "Howling Man"

This 5,000-year-old terracotta figure **(above)** is the largest and most striking relic discovered from the Chalcolithic era, when the island was first settled by humankind. Liquid poured into his gaping mouth (which gives the figure its name) flows down and emerges from his penis. Room 1, Case 1.

Attic Ceramics 2

These painted pots **(right)** and bowls from mainland Greece are clear evidence of trade between ancient Cyprus and the Hellenic world. They depict the hero Theseus and other mythical characters. Room 2.

3 Terracotta Figurines

The earthenware figures in this display represent actors performing the comedies written by Classical Greek playwrights during the 4th and 5th centuries BC. Room 2, Case 3.

NEED TO KNOW

MAP M5 ■ Zinonos Kitieos 4 ■ 24 145 375 ■ www.pierides foundation.com.cy

Open 9am–4pm Mon–Thu, 9am–1pm Fri & Sat

Adm: €3

■ For a cold drink or meal after visiting the museum, cross Zenonos Kitieos Street and walk east to Leoforos Athinon, where you will find a plethora of open-air tavernas and cafés with lovely views of the harbour.

4 The Roman Collection

Almost 400 pieces of delicate and iridescent Roman glassware **(above)** adorn the walls and display cabinets of Room 4.

5 Pomos Heads

These small carved limestone and terracotta heads and figures, found at Pomos on the north-west coast of Cyprus, date from both Greek and Roman times. Among the figures is a bust of the Roman emperor Nero as a young man **(above)**. Room 2.

6 Archaic Pottery

Finds from Margi and Kotsiatis, near Nicosia, include vases and other objects of red and black polished ware from the early Bronze Age (2500–1900 BC). There is also a terracotta idol representing a child in a cradle, and a striking earthenware figurine of the fertility goddess Astarte **(left)**. Room 1, Cases 2–4.

7 Chalkolithic Idols

Visitors can get a glimpse of life in prehistoric times in this part of the museum, which exhibits a rich collection of cruciform idols made from picrolite. These artifacts date back to the Chalkolithic era. However, their religious function is still uncertain.

8 Byzantine and Medieval Ceramics

Sgraffito ware in brown and green glaze, etched with images of animals, birds, warriors, courting couples and a variety of mythical creatures **(right)** are the highlight of this collection. There are also some Byzantine icons. Room 3.

9 Medieval Corridor

Fascinating charts and maps, crusader coats of arms, and ferocious Ottoman scimitars and daggers are displayed in the main corridor.

10 Folklore Wing

This section of the museum contains colourful traditional embroidery, antique lace, silver and amber jewellery, tools, utensils and fine antique furniture.

🔟 ⭐ Ancient Amathous

The foundations of ancient baths, city walls and Byzantine churches can be seen at this evocative hillside archaeological site just outside Limassol. Founded over 3,000 years ago, Amathous was rediscovered during the 19th century, but archaeologists continue to uncover new finds here every year. Amathous's harbour silted up centuries ago and the site is now some distance from the sea. The ruins are illuminated at night throughout the year.

1 Church of the Port

Located to the left of the entrance are the foundations of a very early Christian basilica **(below)**, dating from the 5th century AD.

2 Aqueduct

The aqueduct and an advanced system of mains, reservoirs and sluices were sufficient to supply the whole of ancient Amathous and its citizens with fresh water. The fascinating remains can still be seen at the northwest (upper) corner of the Agora.

3 Gymnasium

Just within the entrance to the site, stone columns mark the location of the Hellenistic gymnasium, where the city's athletes trained and competed.

4 Chapel of Agia Varvara

The walls of this chapel are decorated with frescoes of saints and martyrs, blackened with the smoke of centuries of votive candles.

5 Agora

This expanse of worn limestone slabs **(left)** was the central gathering space and focus of the ancient city. Its size is an indicator of Amathous's importance during its heyday. Some of the columns that surrounded the square have been re-erected.

6 Hellenistic Houses
Excavations continue to take place along this steep, stepped street, which is lined with the walls and foundations of Hellenistic houses and shops **(left)**, and new discoveries are regularly being made.

7 Roman Baths
Between the agora and the original harbour site, geometric mosaics of black and white pebbles were created as the floor of the Roman baths.

8 Acropolis
Parts of the ramparts, which once defended this low hilltop at the heart of the city, survive **(below)**, along with the foundations of a Byzantine basilica and the remains of a temple dedicated to Aphrodite.

The temple of Aphrodite, Amathus

NEED TO KNOW

MAP E6 ■ Coast road, 12 km (7.5 miles) east of Limassol

Open 8:15am–5:15pm daily (to 7:45pm mid-Apr–mid-Sep)

Adm: €2.50

■ To cool off after walking around the site, head for the sea at Agios Georgios Alamanou. The beach is pebbly, but the water is clean and there's a good seafood taverna, Agios Georgios (25 633 634, closed mid-winter).

9 Necropolis
The Necropolis, or Roman cemetery, is on the opposite bank of the Amathous river from the main site. Some of the rock-hewn tombs were re-used later, during the Christian Byzantine era.

10 Medieval Mosaics
Next to the chapel of Agia Varvara, seek out the mosaic floors of the medieval monastery that once stood here. Agia Varvara (St Barbara) is still revered by Greek Orthodox worshippers.

HISTORY OF AMATHOUS

Named for legendary prince Amathous (or, according to another legend, after Amathousa, mother of a king of Pafos), this ancient sea-port flourished from as early as the 10th century BC until the 7th century AD. Raided repeatedly by Saracen corsairs, its harbour fell into disuse, and its end came in 1191, when it was ransacked by Richard the Lionheart – the crusading English king.

Following pages The Selimiye Mosque and the rooftops of Nicosia

■10★ Historic Limassol

This colourful harbour town is Cyprus's second-largest city and at its heart it is a kaleidoscope of architecture, packed with reminders of the island's chequered and multicultural past, from the Crusaders, through the Venetian and Ottoman eras, to the present day. The town's museums are a fine starting point to discover the historical background of the island. Around Limassol's medieval core, the lively streets are authentically Cypriot in character. The best way to explore the historic heart is on foot, and there are plenty of tranquil spots, including the lovely Municipal Gardens, in which to rest.

1 Limassol Marina

The former humble fishermen's harbour (below) has undergone a €300 million facelift and is now a luxurious marina, with top-end restaurants and a prestigious residential area under development.

2 Cyprus Medieval Museum

Inside Limassol Castle, this museum (left) houses armour from the days of the Lusignans, beautiful Byzantine silverware, icons and pottery (see p39).

3 Limassol Castle

This sturdy little stronghold (below) was built by the Lusignan princes on foundations erected by the Byzantines. Later Venetian, Ottoman and British occupiers strengthened its defences.

Map of Historic Limassol

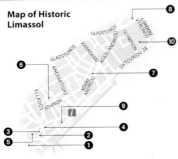

4 Cami Kabir

The graceful minaret of the city's largest mosque **(above)** is a Limassol landmark. It is still used by the city's handful of Turkish Cypriot residents.

5 Lanitis Carob Mill Complex

The former carob mill behind the castle has been tastefully converted into a trendy, multi-use complex. Examples of traditional machinery used in the mill sit among cafés, restaurants, an exhibition space and a micro-brewery.

6 Market Streets

The oldest part of the city is gradually being spruced up. Several streets are lined with market stalls, piled with farm produce and fresh seafood, or displaying attractive traditional crafts.

7 Municipal Folk Art Museum

Housed in a merchant's mansion is a glorious clutter of farm tools, household utensils, silver necklaces and bangles, and traditional village costumes.

8 Limassol Archaeological Museum

A combination of Bronze Age pottery, Roman glassware, gold and jewels from the Classical era, terracotta statuettes, votive offerings and various other finds make this museum worth a visit.

9 Ayia Napa Cathedral

On the fringes of Limassol's old quarter, the cathedral of Ayia Napa **(right)**, with its twin towers and dome, is an example of Orthodox religious architecture at its florid and grandiloquent best.

10 Municipal Gardens

The flowerbeds, trees and fountains of the Municipal Gardens **(left)** are the venue for the city's annual September Wine Festival. The rest of the year this is a quieter spot. It is also home to a mini-zoo.

RICHARD AND BERENGARIA

Princess Berengaria of Navarre was on her way to meet her betrothed, the English king Richard the Lionheart, in Palestine when her ship was forced to take shelter in Limassol. The city was then ruled by the Byzantine prince Isaac Komnenos, who refused Berengaria food and water. In revenge, Richard landed with his army, married Berengaria, and briskly defeated Isaac to claim Cyprus for himself.

NEED TO KNOW

MAP D6

Tourist Office: Spyrou Araouzou; 25 362 756

Limassol Castle and Medieval Museum: off Irinis; 25 305 419. Open: 8am–5pm Mon–Fri, 9am–5pm Sat, 10am–1pm Sun. Adm: €4.50

Limassol Archaeological Museum: Anastasi Sioukri and Vyronos; 25 305 157. Open: 8am–4pm Mon–Fri. Adm: €2.50

Municipal Folk Art Museum: Agiou Andreou 253; 25 362 303. Open: 7:45am–2:45pm Mon–Fri. Adm: €2

Cami Kabir: Open: 9am–4pm daily (closed at prayer times)

■ Don't miss the great view of the town from the roof terrace of the castle.

🔟 ⭐ Kourion

Looking out over the Mediterranean from its cliff top, Kourion is the most spectacularly located ancient site in Cyprus. First settled by the Mycenaeans, the city reached its apogee in Roman times, evidenced by remnants of the empire including its great stadium, theatre and lavish public baths. As in many of Cyprus's greatest ancient cities, the cults of Aphrodite and Apollo thrived in Kourion, and both of these Hellenistic deities have shrines here. Wandering through Kourion's ruins, it is not hard to imagine the city as it must once have been: one of the jewels of Rome's eastern possessions, until its destruction by an earthquake in 365 AD.

1 Roman Theatre
Now completely restored, the theatre **(left)**, with its columns and tiers of seats, and magnificent sea views, is a summer venue for a range of performances, from Greek music to Shakespeare plays.

2 Roman Baths
Splendid mosaics dating from the Christian era, depicting fish, birds and flowers, decorate the floors of the Roman baths and the adjoining villa of Eustolios. Also visible is the highly sophisticated hypocaust – underfloor heating – system.

3 Roman Agora and Nymphaeum
The graceful 2nd century AD pillars of the Roman agora, or marketplace **(below)**, and the nymphaeum, which was originally a huge public fountain, can still be seen.

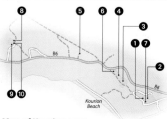

Map of Kourion area

4 House of the Gladiators
This Roman villa is named after its mosaics **(below)** of gladiators in armed combat who fought in the arena.

GREEK DEITIES
Along with Aphrodite, who is said to have come ashore on the island, the sun-god Apollo is the Greek deity most associated with Cyprus. His cult had its beginnings as Apollo Kereates and was established as that of Apollo Hylates by the 3rd century BC. However, when Christianity came to Cyprus many of his sacred sites were taken over as places of worship.

5 Roman Stadium
This hillside stadium, discovered by archaeologists in 1939, could seat as many as 6,000 spectators. It fell into disuse after Kourion was abandoned in the 5th century AD.

6 House of Achilles
Next to the House of the Gladiators, this villa had a striking floor mosaic of Odysseus and Achilles, the Greek heroes of Homer's saga of the Trojan War, and of the rape of the youth Ganymede by the god Zeus.

7 Annexe of Eustolios
This 4th century AD villa was owned by a wealthy Christian. It features beautiful floor mosaics of birds, fish and Ktisis, the female spirit of creation, who is seen holding a ruler.

8 Treasury of Apollo
Close to the Temple of Apollo is the sacred Treasury where priests made votive offerings to the god Apollo. Next to it are the remnants of a shrine dating from the 8th century BC.

9 Sanctuary of Apollo Ylatis
Standing above and to the west of Kourion, this complex of temples and shrines **(main image/below)** was sacred to the sun-god Apollo. Many of its ancient walls and columns have been re-erected.

10 Circular Monument
Ritual processions and sacred dances were held around the holy trees planted in seven rock pits surrounded by this circular mosaic pavement. The monument is unique in Cyprus but similar ones have been found in other parts of the world.

NEED TO KNOW

MAP C6 ■ 19 km (12 miles) west of Limassol ■ 25 934 250

Open 8:15am–5:15pm daily (to 7:45pm mid-Apr–mid-Sep) ■ Adm €4.50

Sanctuary of Apollo Ylatis: 3 km (1.5 miles) west of Kourion.

Opening times same as the Kourion site; combined admission tickets for both

■ About 3 km (1.5 miles) from the Kourion site is the village of Episkopi, which has several restaurants and the Kourion Archaeological Museum (Open 8am–3pm Mon–Fri; Adm: €2.50).

■ The best time to visit Kourion is early in the day, before the numerous tour groups arrive.

⭐ Troödos Painted Churches

At first sight, it is hard to believe that these unassuming little stone buildings conceal such glories behind their mossy walls. Yet the isolated Troödos churches are the guardians of a unique treasury of Byzantine religious art and some of the most superb early Christian frescoes in the world. Since being given UNESCO World Heritage status in the 1980s, many have been restored.

1 Panagia tou Moutoulla

One of the oldest of the Troödos churches (1280), this chapel of the Virgin **(below)** has frescoes of St George and St Christopher – both in Byzantine armour – and of the Virgin and infant Christ. Unrestored, they are rare and important works.

2 Agios Ioannis Lampadistis

The three churches located within this monastery have fresco sequences from the 13th to the 15th centuries.

3 Agios Nikolaos tis Stegis

One of the oldest Cypriot churches dedicated to St Nicholas, this former monastery chapel features some beautiful frescoes **(right)** from the 11th to the 15th centuries.

4 Metamorfosi tou Sotirou

This early 16th-century chapel is decorated with beautiful yet unusual frescoes featuring scenes from the life of Christ.

5 Archangelos Michael

The frescoes of this village church **(left)**, dating from 1474, are more lively than some of their rivals. Their colours were brightened by restorations in 1980 and 2008 and include a range of Gospel and Old Testament scenes.

6 Panagia tou Araka

The rather melancholy portrait of Christ *Pantokrator* **(left)**, dating from 1192, in the dome of this church is finely preserved. It is surrounded by fresco portraits of the 12 Old Testament prophets and, near the apse, the Annunciation and Presentation of Christ.

Map of Troödos church sites

7 Panagia tis Podithou

Dramatic depictions of the Crucifixion and the Virgin are the most striking feature of this 16th-century church, surrounded by fields and woodland.

8 Stavros tou Agiasmati

Cleaned and restored to their pristine colours the frescoes **(right)**, of this 15th-century church are by the religious painter Philippos Goul. The most striking, decorating the full round of the ceiling, are scenes from the Gospels, including The Last Supper, Peter's Denial and the Assumption.

PHILIPPOS GOUL

The finest frescoes in the Troödos churches are the work of the late 15th-century icon painter Philippos (or Philip) Goul. His speciality was the depiction of Old Testament prophets and events, as well as the all-seeing Christ *Pantokrator* (the Almighty). Many Troödos churches lack the domed roof typical of Greek Orthodox places of worship, and painters such as Goul and his apprentices had to adapt their style to suit the unique architecture of sloping roofs and walls.

9 Panagia Forviotissa

The Church of Our Lady of the Meadows stands on its own on a wooded hillside **(above)**. The interior boasts a 12th-century nave and frescoes painted between then and the early 16th century.

10 Timios Stavros (Holy Cross)

This small 14th-century church has a unique icon of Christ with the Virgin Mary and John the Baptist, and fine Byzantine- and Venetian-influenced wall paintings.

NEED TO KNOW

MAP C4 ■ Cyprus Tourism Information Office: Platres, 25 421 316

Panagia tou Moutoulla: Open: dawn–dusk daily (contact the village coffee shop)

Agios Ioannis Lampadistis: Open: 8am–1pm & 2–7pm Tue–Sat (Nov–Apr: to 4pm), 10am–1pm & 2–4pm Sun

Agios Nikolaos tis Stegis: Open: 9am–4pm Tue–Sat, 11am–4pm Sun

Archangelos Michael: Open: 10am–6pm daily

Panagia Forviotissa: Open: 9:30am–4pm Mon–Sat, 10am–4pm Sun & public hols

■ Contact the closest coffee house to gain access to churches not listed above.

TOP 10 ⭐ Kato Pafos Archaeological Park

The most accessible, exciting and inspiring archaeological site on the island, the ruins at Kato Pafos were first unearthed as recently as 1962, shedding dramatic new light on Cyprus under the Roman Empire. Now a UNESCO World Heritage Site, the remains discovered here span more than 2,000 years. The lavish mosaics found on the floors of four Roman villas indicate that this was a place of ostentatious wealth in its glory days. Some display saucy scenes of deities and mortals carousing – an indication, perhaps, that Cyprus was as much a pleasure seeker's island then as it is now.

Saranda Kolones ❶

This stronghold was built by 13th-century Lusignan kings on the remnants of a Byzantine castle. Its massive, battered walls **(right)** and honeycomb of vaults and dungeons are ringed by a dry moat.

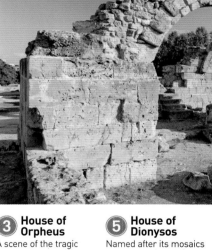

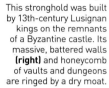

❷ Villa of Theseus

The villa **(above)** is named after its superb mosaics, in which a heroic, club-wielding Theseus prepares to take on the Minotaur, watched by Ariadne. Achilles, champion of the siege of Troy, is shown as an infant.

❸ House of Orpheus

A scene of the tragic musician Orpheus pacifying a menagerie of savage beasts is the highlight of the mosaics here. The building, however, is closed to the public.

❺ House of Dionysos

Named after its mosaics of Dionysos **(below)**, the god of wine, this is the largest of the four opulent villas found at Kato Pafos.

House of Aion ❹

Hermes and the god Dionysos features in the mosaics in this villa, unearthed in 1983 and dating from the 4th century AD. Other scenes show the god Apollo, the legendary royal beauty Cassiopeia and the god Aion, after whom the building is named.

6 Asklipion
The Asklipion was sacred to Asklipios, god of medicine. It was a hospital and a temple and its priests were renowned for their healing skills.

8 Roman Odeon
The partly restored Roman odeon **(above)**, with its 11 tiers of seats, stands on a hillside overlooking the rest of the site. Built in the early 2nd century AD, it was levelled by an earthquake three centuries later.

9 Agora
The marketplace was the hub of the city's social, political and commercial life and was originally surrounded by a grand colonnade.

10 Hellenistic Theatre
Overlooking Kato Pafos from the south slope of Fabrica Hill, this semi-circular theatre **(below)** has many rows of stone benches, cut into the rock.

7 Roman Walls
Long ramparts and a moat protected Kato Pafos during its heyday as one of the wealthiest cities in Roman Cyprus.

Map of Kato Pafos Archaeological Park

LEOF. APOSTOLOU PAVLOU

POSEIDONOS

Pafos Harbour

NEED TO KNOW

MAP A5 ▪ 26 306 217

Open 8:30am–5pm daily (to 7:30pm mid-Apr–mid-Sep) ▪ Adm: €4.50

▪ Bring plenty of bottled water with you as there are no refreshment facilities on the site.

▪ There's a large, free car park on the inland side of Apostolou Pavlou Street, directly opposite the harbour.

▪ For a panoramic view, climb to the roof of the miniature Frankish-Ottoman castle, which guards the harbour.

Akamas Peninsula

The Akamas region is southern Cyprus's last and least developed frontier – a region of spectacular, rugged scenery, sandy coves where turtles nest and dolphins occasionally frolic, clear water, quaint villages and extensive vineyards, which support the local wine industry. If empty beaches are what you seek, the Akamas has them, and more: ancient Stone Age dwellings, remnants of Byzantine and Classical settlements and starkly beautiful sea cliffs on the westernmost extremity of the island.

Agios Georgios and Cape Drepano ①
Atop the headland of Cape Drepano, mosaics of sea creatures adorn the floors of what was once a large Byzantine cathedral **(right)**.

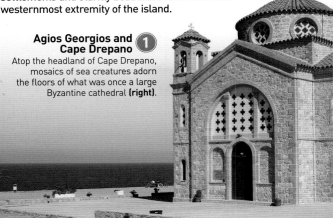

② Lempa Neolithic Village
Lempa was home to the earliest islanders, who settled here more than 5,500 years ago. Archaeologists have rebuilt dwellings dating from the Chalkolithic era.

③ Baths of Aphrodite
According to legend, this pool **(above)** is where the goddess bathed after entertaining her paramours. It is said that if you drink from its waters you will fall for the next person you see. Visitors are not allowed in the pool.

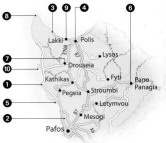

Map of Akamas Peninsula

Lakki, Polis, Lysos, Drouseia, Fyti, Pano Panagia, Kathikas, Stroumbi, Pegeia, Letymvou, Mesogi, Pafos

④ Polis
This fast-developing resort still oozes a certain laid-back charm. A small archaeological museum displays relics of the ancient settlement of Arsinoe and Marion, either side of the present-day village, and the small church of Agios Andronikos has some fine frescoes.

🔟 Moments in History

1 Prehistoric Cyprus

Neolithic people settled in Cyprus over 10,000 years ago. By 3900 BC copper tools were in use and by 2500 BC Cyprus was part of a Bronze Age civilization with links to Egypt, Asia Minor and the Aegean. In the 12th century BC Achaean Greeks began to oust the original Eteocypriot inhabitants.

2 Geometric, Archaic and Classical Periods

By 1050 BC there were ten city-states and a flourishing cult of Aphrodite. The wealth of Cyprus lured Phoenicians, who settled at Kition, as well as Assyrian, Egyptian and Persian invaders. In 333 BC Alexander the Great added Cyprus to his empire.

3 Hellenistic Era

After Alexander's death Cyprus fell to the Ptolemaic dynasty of Alexandria until 58 BC, when the island was annexed by Rome. The Apostles Paul and Barnabas converted Sergius Paulus, the Roman proconsul of Cyprus, to Christianity in AD 45.

Nikephoros Phokas

4 Byzantine Era

From AD 330 Cyprus was ruled by Constantinople. Earthquakes destroyed coastal cities in the 4th century, but otherwise it was a period of peace. From the mid-7th century the island was devastated by Arab pirates who were not defeated by Emperor Nikephoros Phokas until 965.

5 The Lusignans

Richard the Lionheart of England seized Cyprus from the Byzantines in 1191 and sold it to the Knights Templar, who in turn sold it to Guy de Lusignan, exiled King of Jerusalem. The Roman Catholic Church supplanted the Greek Orthodox faith.

6 The Venetians

Venice acquired Cyprus in 1489 from the widow of the last Lusignan king, and fortified both Nicosia and Famagusta against the Ottomans, but in 1571 the island finally fell to the Ottomans.

7 The Ottomans

The Turks restored the Orthodox faith whilst encouraging conversion to Islam. Cyprus was seen as a backwater until 1878, when Britain took over in return for supporting Turkey against Russia. In 1914 Britain formally annexed Cyprus.

8 Independent Cyprus

Cyprus won independence from Britain on 16 August 1960 after a violent national liberation struggle by Greek Cypriots. However, friction between the Greek and Turkish Cypriot communities continued and in 1974 Athens engineered a coup

Fresco depicting Apostle Barnabas

Signing the Treaty of Independence

against the Cypriot government with the aim of uniting Cyprus with Greece, while Turkey invaded to protect Turkish Cypriots. Since a ceasefire, the "Attila Line", patrolled by UN troops, divides the Turkish-occupied north from the south.

9 Divided Cyprus

In 1983 the northern part of the island declared itself independent as the Turkish Republic of Northern Cyprus (TRNC). It was, and continues to be, recognized only by Turkey.

Northern Cyprus, with the Turkish flag

10 EU Membership

In April 2003 the Turkish Cypriot authorities allowed free movement by Greek Cypriots and visitors to the north of the island. Members of both communities now regularly visit the "other side". On 1 May, 2004, the Republic of Cyprus was made a full member of the European Union. In 2013, it suffered an economic crisis which led to a series of austerity measures. Recently there have been cautious signs of recovery.

TOP 10 HISTORICAL FIGURES

1 Evagoras of Salamis
Evagoras (410–374 BC), king of the city-state of Salamis, conquered much of Cyprus, but was defeated when rival city Amathous allied itself with the Persian Empire.

2 Alexander the Great
Cyprus welcomed the great military leader Alexander as a liberator from Persian dominance in 333 BC.

3 Apostle Barnabas
Apostle Barnabas, with Apostle Paul, brought Christianity to Cyprus in 45 AD.

4 Nikephoros Phokas
The Byzantine emperor (963–9) drove the Saracen corsairs from Cyprus.

5 Richard the Lionheart
When the ship carrying Richard's fiancée was driven by storms to Limassol, the English king (1157–99) seized Cyprus (see p25).

6 Guy de Lusignan
Driven from the throne of Jerusalem, Guy established the Kingdom of Cyprus and ruled until his death in 1194.

7 Peter I
The Lusignan ruler (1358–69) led a series of successful military attacks in the eastern Mediterranean, until he was assassinated by three of his own knights.

8 Selim the Sot
The Muslim sultan drove the Venetians from Cyprus after a 10-month siege.

9 Hadjigeorgiakis Kornesios
This interpreter between Ottoman rulers and the outside world became the richest man in Cyprus, until he was beheaded in 1809.

10 Archbishop Makarios
Makarios (1913–77) led the campaign for independence and was the first president of the Republic of Cyprus.

Archbishop Makarios

🔟 Galleries and Museums

Sealife display at the Thalassa Museum, Ayia Napa

1 Cyprus Museum, Nicosia

This is the most important museum in Cyprus, with a treasury of archaeological finds and historic relics from the Neolithic era to the end of the Roman Empire. Among the exhibits are ancient ceramics, superb jewellery and sculptures (see pp14–15).

2 Byzantine Museum and Art Galleries, Nicosia

MAP Q2 ▪ Archbishop Makarios III Foundation, Plateia Archiepiskopou Kyprianou ▪ Open 9am–4:30pm Mon–Fri, 9am–1pm Sat ▪ Dis. access ▪ Adm

The magnificent early Christian Kanakaria mosaics are the gem of this museum, which also has exquisite late-Byzantine frescoes that were stolen and later recovered. There is also a collection of icons.

Fresco, Byzantine Museum

3 Thalassa Museum, Ayia Napa

Kryou Nerou 14 ▪ 23 816 366 ▪ Open Oct–May: 9am–1pm Mon, 9am–5pm Tue–Sat; Jun–Sep: 9am–1pm, 6–10pm Mon, 9am–5pm Tue–Sat, 9am–1pm Sun ▪ Dis. access ▪ Adm

This fascinating museum hosts sea-related artifacts dating from prehistoric times to the late 19th century. A replica of the Kyrenia Ship, the original of which is in Kyrenia Castle, has pride of place.

4 Leventis Municipal Museum, Nicosia

MAP P3 ▪ Ippokratous 17 ▪ Open 10am–4:30pm Tue–Sun

This award-winning museum, set in an old town house, offers a glimpse of Nicosia from ancient times to 1900 with its display of prehistoric artifacts, Lusignan pottery, old engravings and posters. There are also exhibits on long-vanished trades and crafts.

5 AG Leventis Gallery

MAP N3 ▪ AG Leventis (ex Leonidou) 5 ▪ 22 668 838 ▪ Open 10am–5pm Mon & Thu–Sun (to 10pm Wed) ▪ Dis. access ▪ Adm

This striking museum in the newer part of town displays work mainly by European painters from the 16th–20th centuries, as well as Cypriot artists. It is the former private collection of the late Anastosios Leventis, a wealthy Cypriot businessman.

⑥ Pierides Foundation, Larnika

The oldest private museum on the island houses an eclectic collection of ancient and Byzantine treasures, as well as examples of local crafts and traditional costumes (see pp18–19).

⑦ Agios Lazaros Byzantine Museum, Larnaka

MAP M6 ▪ Plateia Agiou Lazarou ▪ Open 8:30am–12:30pm, 3–5:30pm Mon–Sat (closed Wed & Sat pm)

Within the Church of St Lazaros are displays of 18th- and 19th-century ecclesiastical silver, as well as carved wooden doors and ships' figureheads.

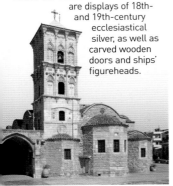

Agios Lazaros Byzantine Museum

⑧ Larnaka Archaeological Museum

Among the highlights here are a reconstructed tomb from Neolithic Choirokoitia, Bronze Age pottery and a fish-shaped wine goblet (see p78).

⑨ Larnaka Municipal Art Gallery

MAP M5 ▪ Plateia Evropis ▪ Open 9am–4pm Mon–Fri, 10am–1pm Sat ▪ Dis. access

Five restored warehouses host exhibitions by Cypriot and foreign artists.

⑩ Cyprus Medieval Museum, Limassol

MAP D6 ▪ Irinis ▪ Open 8am–5pm Mon–Fri, 9am–5pm Sat, 10am–1pm Sun ▪ Adm

In Limassol's castle, this collection features Lusignan swords, Byzantine silver and ceramics, and fine icons.

TOP 10 UNUSUAL MUSEUMS

Classic Motorcycle Museum

1 Municipal Museum of Paleontology, Larnaka
MAP M5 ▪ Plateia Evropis
▪ Open Tue–Sun
Shells and fossils.

2 Museum of Cypriot Coinage, Strovolos
MAP F3 ▪ Stasinou 51
▪ Open Mon–Fri
Ancient coins.

3 Cyprus Postal Museum, Nicosia
MAP F3 ▪ Agiou Savva 3B
▪ Open Mon–Sat
Philatelic phenomena.

4 Museum of the Liberation Struggle, Nicosia
MAP Q2 ▪ Apost. Varnava
▪ Open Mon–Fri
History of independence.

5 Fyti Village Weaving Museum
MAP B4 ▪ Open Mon–Sat
Handwoven textiles and weaving.

6 Cyprus Classic Motorcycle Museum, Nicosia
MAP F3 ▪ Granikou St
▪ Open Mon–Sat ▪ Adm
Motorcycles.

7 Marine Life Museum, Ayia Napa
MAP J4 ▪ Agias Mavris 25
▪ Open Mon–Sat ▪ Adm
Stuffed sharks and seafaring vessels.

8 Lefkara Museum of Traditional Embroidery
MAP E5 ▪ Open daily ▪ Adm
Lace and silverware.

9 Naive Sculpture Museum, Mazotos
MAP F5 ▪ Open daily ▪ Adm
Village life.

10 Oleastro, Anogyra
MAP C5 ▪ Open daily ▪ Adm
Olive production.

TOP10 **Monasteries and Convents**

1 Machairas Monastery

Picturesquely located and sensitively restored, Machairas was founded in 1148. The centuries-old monks' cells, stables and cellars are fascinating, and there is a fine collection of superbly executed and well-preserved icons (see p74).

Machairas Monastery

2 Stavrovouni Monastery

Offering awesome views from its hilltop location, this monastery was founded in the 4th century by St Helena, mother of Emperor Constantine I, and is named the "Mountain of the Cross". It is said to house a fragment of the Holy Cross, and its monks keep strict vows based on the rules of Mt Athos in Greece. Women are not allowed to enter (see p79).

3 Agios Irakleidos Convent

An air of age-old mystery hovers over this early monastery, founded in AD 400 in honour of Irakleidos. He welcomed the Apostles Paul and Barnabas to Cyprus, who brought with them Christianity, and he became the first Bishop of Tamassos. His bones are displayed in an ornate silver reliquary. The monastery is now run by nuns (see p74).

4 Agios Minas Convent

MAP E5 ■ Open May–Sep: 8am–noon, 3–5pm daily; Oct–Apr: 8am–noon, 2–5pm daily

Graceful white cloisters surround a small 15th-century church and house a community of nuns, whose fine painted icons are much sought after by collectors.

5 Panagia tis Amasgou

MAP D5 ■ Open dawn–dusk daily

Some wonderful – but unrestored – frescoes dating from the 12th to the 16th centuries are the must-see feature of this nunnery church. It is the only Byzantine building located in the Kouris Valley, near Limassol.

6 Panagia tou Sinti Monastery

MAP B5

Standing alone on the banks of the Xeros, Panagia tou Sinti is deserted and a little ghostly. Founded in the 16th century, it is one of the island's most important Venetian buildings, and has been awarded the Europa Nostra prize for the sensitive restoration work carried out in the 1990s. The monastery, however, is kept locked.

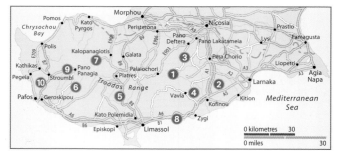

Ornate interior of the Kykkos Monastery

7 **Kykkos Monastery**
MAP C4 ■ Open Jun–Oct:
10am–6pm daily; Nov–May: 10am–
4pm daily ■ Adm (treasury)

This 900-year-old shrine guards a legendary, miracle-working icon of the Virgin Mary. Given to the monastery's founder, the hermit Isaiah, by Emperor Alexios Komnenos, it has been hidden from profane eyes for centuries and remains so to this day. Kykkos is one of the great centres of the Orthodox faith and still attracts pilgrims from all over the world.

Agios Georgios Alamanos Convent

8 **Agios Georgios Alamanos Convent**
MAP E6 ■ Open dawn–dusk daily

Lovingly tended flower and herb gardens surround this small convent, which was founded almost 900 years ago. They are cultivated by a small community of nuns, who also paint attractive icons and make and sell their own honey here.

9 **Chrysorrogiatissa Monastery**

The monks of this impressive monastery, devoted to "Our Lady of the Golden Pomegranate" (an attribute of Aphrodite), guard a treasury of icons and costly religious ornaments which have been hoarded here since its foundation in the 12th century (see p94). These include an icon of the Virgin Mary, discovered by St Ignatios, and kept on the iconostasis. The monks also make some of Cyprus's finest vintages on the premises, and these can be tasted and bought at their winery, Monte Royia (see p63).

10 **Agios Neofytos Monastery**
MAP B5 ■ Open Apr–Oct: 9am–
1pm, 2–6pm daily; Nov–Mar:
9am–4pm daily ■ Adm

The elaborate iron crowns and silken vestments of Orthodox bishops are among the highlights of this monastery's museum. Equally fascinating are the frescoes in its cave-like chapel, a grotto dug by Neofytos, the hermit who founded it in the late 12th century.

🔟 Scenic Villages

1 Vavla
MAP E5

With its mellow old stone houses in varying states of disrepair, picturesque Vavla stands among rolling hills with lovely views of the Troödos Mountains. A world away from all the coastal tourist hype.

2 Kalavasos

This lively village, with great views of the mountains, is centred around a lavishly decorated church. Kalavasos also makes an ideal base for exploring the Neolithic remains of a roundhouse and tombs at nearby Tenta, and for walks, hikes, bicycle rides and horseriding in the surrounding countryside *(see p80)*.

Traditional red-tiled house, Fikardou

3 Tochni

Set in a valley amid lush olive groves and vineyards, Tochni is a tranquil village built around a picturesque church. With several sunny tavernas and cafés to choose from, it's a good place to pause for refreshment, particularly after visiting the Neolithic settlement at Choirokoitia or the Agios Minas Monastery, both of which are nearby *(see p80)*.

4 Fikardou

Fikardou *(see p74)* has won a Europa Nostra award for its unique preservation of Cypriot village life and architecture. Some 40 restored houses, climbing the hillside, retain their traditional red-tiled roofs, mud brick and stone walls, while two 18th-century homes – the Katsinioros and Achilleas Dimitri houses – function as a rural museum.

The pretty church of Agiou Konstantinou and Elenis, Tochni

5 Kakopetria

The name of this village high in the northern Troödos foothills means "the evil rockpile". It was so named by the original settlers who had to clear boulders off the ridge to build the village. Attractively restored ancient stone houses and an old-fashioned watermill add to its charm (see p104).

Picturesque Kalopanagiotis

6 Kalopanagiotis
MAP C4

The valley view is the chief charm of this little village, along with UNESCO-listed frescoed monastery. In addition, there are some fine old-fashioned mansions, as well as a couple of graceful Venetian bridges spanning fast-running streams. There are good walking trails nearby.

7 Fyti
MAP B4

Looking down over slopes and fields to the beaches of the west coast, Fyti is an old-fashioned spot, best known for making lace, textiles and woven wall-hangings (see p39).

8 Lofou
MAP C5

The sleepy village of Lofou is set on vine-studded hilltops in the Troödos foothills. It is dazzlingly pretty, with clumps of bougainvillea and morning glory hanging from its historic buildings, most of which have been restored.

9 Monagri
MAP D5

Picturesque Monagri is well worth a visit to see the nearby 18th-century monastic church of Archangelos. The church features contemporary frescoes by painter Filaretos, a geometric mihrab decoration from the period when it was used as a mosque, and pillars salvaged from a Roman temple.

10 Silikou
MAP D5

Breathtakingly scenic, Silikou is still a working village, not just a tourist spot. Set amid olive groves, there is an olive oil museum displaying traditional tools and techniques.

Olive groves surround Silikou

🔟 Beaches

① Coral Bay

Kolpos ton Koralion, located only 8 km (5 miles) north of Pafos, is known by everyone as Coral Bay. The sweep of fine sand, covered by rows of sunbeds all summer, makes it a popular destination among young Cypriots from Larnaka and Limassol *(see p95)*.

Crystal-clear waters at Coral Bay

② Ayia Napa

The beaches of Ayia Napa are among the finest in southern Cyprus – and the liveliest, with activities ranging from water-skiiing to bungee jumping and quad-bike riding. Nissi is the closest to town, and gets busy in high summer. Makronissos, longer and less crowded, is 5 km (3 miles) from the town centre, while Kyro Nero extends east from the fishing harbour *(see pp16–17)*.

③ Evdimou

Despite sea and sand as clean and clear as any along the south coast, Evdimou is uncrowded and undeveloped, save for tavernas at each end *(see p95)*.

④ Pissouri Bay

Pissouri is another great beach on the southern coast and is popular with families, water-skiers and wind-surfers. There are several places to eat and drink along the beach and at Pissouri village inland *(see p95)*.

⑤ Pafos

Pafos's best beaches are on the eastern edge of town, near Geroskipou, where the Cyprus Tourism Organization maintains a family-friendly strand, and still further east at Floria Beach, next to Pafos airport. Close to the centre of Kato Pafos, there is also a municipal beach at Vrysoudia, with loungers and umbrellas for hire, and a small café *(see p95)*.

⑥ Lara Bay

Superb beaches lie on each side of Cape Lara. South of the cape, there's almost 2 km (1 mile) of uncrowded sand, while to the north *(see p95)* there's a shallow bay frequented by loggerhead turtles *(see p33)*. The turtle protection group arranges occasional night-time walks along the beach in egg-laying season, when you can watch the turtles struggling ashore. After laying, the eggs are carefully removed to a protected area on the beach where they are safe from dogs, foxes and other predators.

⑦ Governor's Beach

A string of small bays of black sand offset by white cliffs, Governor's Beach is a favourite with Cypriots getting away from it all, with plenty of snack-bars and tavernas, sunbeds to rent and water sports *(see p95)*.

White cliffs at Governor's Beach

Water sports on the white-sand beach at Protaras

8 Protaras

"Fig Tree Bay", this resort's favourite beach, has fine white sand and tropical turquoise sea, and is usually a little less hectic than the youth-orientated strands at Ayia Napa, only 5 km (3 miles) away. In Protaras itself a range of water sports are available *(see p81)*.

9 Asprokremmos

Those seeking Cyprus's best uncrowded beach need look no further than this super stretch of sand extending west from Lakki *(see p95)*.

10 Polis

A long sand-and-pebble beach stretches eastwards along Chrysochou Bay *(see p95)*, which is

a 15-minute walk from the centre of Polis – the fastest-growing little resort in western Cyprus. There are less-crowded stretches of sand and shingle to the west of the village, too. If you're hungry there is a pleasant open-air bar-restaurant and a picnic area beneath eucalyptus trees.

Pretty Chrysochou Bay, near Polis

🔟 Water Sports

Sailing off the Cyprus coast

1 Sailing

Skippered yachts can be chartered from island marinas (Larnaka and Limassol are the main centres) by the day or for longer cruises, and smaller dinghies and catamarans are available by the day or half-day from beaches around Ayia Napa, Protaras and Lakki.

2 "Banana" Rides

Bright yellow inflatable "bananas" towed at speed by motor boats can carry half a dozen or so passengers. The challenge is to stay aboard while the boat's movement makes the "banana" perform an increasingly extreme series of aquatic maneouvres. Life jackets are essential and most operators insist on an over-15s only policy.

3 Swimming

Cyprus's sea is crystal clear, clean and ideal for swimming. Most beaches have lifeguards on duty in high season, but look out for red flags, which mean bathing is inadvisable at that time because of high waves or strong currents. Most holiday hotels have at least one large outdoor pool for serious swimmers and a smaller pool for toddlers, but only a few deluxe hotels have indoor pools for use in winter.

4 Open Sea Fishing

There are over 250 species of fish living in the warm waters off the coast of Cyprus and many fishing villages hire out boats and organize fishing excursions. Refreshments are usually served on board and you can take your catch home at the end of the day. In Northern Cyprus, Kyrenia is the main centre for deep-sea fishing trips.

5 Windsurfing and Kiteboarding

Ayia Napa and Protaras have the best conditions for windsurfing and kite-boarding. Boards can be rented by day or half-day at many of the island's resort hotels and public beaches. The best time of day for both sports is usually mid- to late

Windsurfer

afternoon when a light breeze tends to spring up.

6 Jetskiing

Bouncing from wave to wave on the back of a motorized "waterbike" is a popular beach pastime for locals as well as visitors. Jetskis can be hired at all resort beaches but, due to the cost of fuel, it's a relatively expensive activity. Lifejackets are compulsory and it's essential to steer well clear of the lines of coloured buoys designating swimmer-only stretches of inshore water.

Challenging "Banana" Rides

8 Waterskiing

Limassol, Larnaka and Ayia Napa are the best spots for waterskiing, for beginners as well as for experts, because the sea tends to be calmer at these locations. You will find dozens of competing water-ski outfits at each resort that will supply all the necessary gear and take you out on the water, so shop around for the best price.

9 Snorkelling

There is always plenty to see underwater, even within a few yards of the shore if you are a beginner at this sport. The shallows teem with tiny fish, while sea anemones and urchins cling to the rocks and, if you are lucky, you may even see an octopus slithering past. Stronger swimmers should head out to the rocky shores where there is more to see than on the sandy bottom *(see pp48–9)*. One of the best places for snorkelling in Cyprus is the north coast of the Akamas Peninsula *(see pp32–3)*, where countless rocky coves and tiny islands not too far offshore abound in a variety of sea life, including larger fish such as grouper.

Scuba diving off the coast of Cyprus

7 Scuba Diving

Splendid underwater visibility makes Cyprus one of the best diving destinations in the Mediterranean, with some highly rated wreck dives and plenty of professional diving centres. The best diving is off the west coast, and there are dives at all depths and for all levels of expertise. There are PADI and British Sub Aqua Club-approved dive-training centres at all the major resorts *(see pp48–9)*.

10 Parascending

You don't need any special skills to strap on a parachute harness and soar into the air as you are pulled along by a fast-moving speedboat, but you do need a certain amount of nerve. The rewards are a splendid bird's-eye view of your resort and an exhilarating ride. Most resorts have outlets offering this fun activity.

Thrill-seekers enjoy parascending across Cypriot waters

🔟 Diving and Snorkelling Sites

1 Wreck of the Vera K
Sunk during World War II, part of this Lebanese freighter's hull lies in only 8 m (26 ft) of water, near the Moulia Rocks just offshore Geroskipou Beach. It is surrounded by shell casings and amphorae and the wreck attracts plenty of fish. An excellent dive for beginners.

2 Wreck of the Zenobia
This 170-m (555-ft) Swedish truck ferry went down off the coast at Larnaka in 1980 on her maiden voyage (no lives were lost) and lies 43 m (140 ft) underwater. Today it is considered the best wreck dive in the Mediterranean and many claim that it is also one of the best in the world. More than 100 cargo lorries can all be seen, fully intact, and the wreck offers good diving opportunities at all levels. Abundant marine life can be seen around the wreck, including grouper, tuna, conger eels and barracuda. More advanced divers can also descend deeper to explore other interesting parts of the vessel's interior, such as the engine room.

Atmospheric wreck of the Achilleas

3 Wreck of the Achilleas
Mystery still surrounds the wrecking of the *Achilleas*, which blew up not far from the shore and sank in 1975 in 11 m (36 ft) of water. The wreck is in three sections, at varying depths, and is frequented by silvery hordes of smaller sea denizens. Grouper and even a moray or two can also be seen around the ship from time to time.

4 Mismaloya Reef
The Mismaloya Reef abounds in shoals of bass and bream, as well as larger pelagic species. One of the remoter dive sites from Pafos,

Wreck of the Zenobia – the best dive site in the Mediterranean

it takes longer to reach and is more suitable for experienced divers and those who don't mind spending some time at sea.

5 Wreck of the Ektimon

This is an excellent beginner's dive, in only 6 m (19 ft) of water. The *Ektimon* itself, a Greek freighter which ran aground in 1971, has almost disintegrated, but its propellers still mark the spot.

6 St George's Island

Just off the northwest coast, in the Akamas Marine Reserve, the slopes of this rocky islet abound in marine life, including moray and grouper. You can descend to 35 m (115 ft) to explore underwater caves. Sheltered from the westerly winds, St George's is a good alternative when west coast sites are not diveable due to high seas or poor visibility.

Coral off the coast of Cyprus

St George's Island

7 Jubilee Shoals

For experienced divers, these shallows, some 35 km (22 miles) offshore in the Pafos area, are a great place to see large pelagics such as tuna and jack, as well as octopus and moray. The site consists of a vast underwater cliff, with caves, pinnacles and a tunnel. Dives offer drop-offs from the 20-m (82-ft) to 60-m (197-ft) levels. This site takes longer to get to than most Cyprus dives but is an unmissable experience if you have the qualifications.

8 Amphorae Caves

This is a fascinating offshore cave dive – the clay wine-jars that are embedded in the roof of one

of the caves seem to imply, according to archaeologists, that the caves and gullies were once above the waterline and have been drowned over the past two thousand years by seismic movement. Beautiful coral abounds here. The maximum depth is 10 m (33 ft).

9 Wall Street

This dive involves a plunge into a long, narrow gulley with a profusion of sponges, anemones, soft corals and lots of smaller marine life in depths of 25–30 m (82–98 ft). It is a relatively easy dive, and therefore suitable for beginners, but it still offers a spectacular introduction to the underwater world of Cypriot seas.

10 Petra Gialias

This is a shallow dive set around large offshore boulders. Surrounding these rocks the sea bed attracts huge shoals of smaller fish, as well as the occasional octopus or larger fish such as grouper and barracuda.

🔟 Activities on Land

A hiking trail in Akamas Peninsula

1 Mountain Walking
Walking through the cool forests and rugged valleys of the Troödos brings you closer to Cyprus's natural beauty and wildlife than any other way of exploring the island. Spring and autumn are the best times to head for the hills.

2 Tennis
Keen tennis fans will find all-weather, floodlit public courts all over Cyprus, and within most five-star hotels and apartment complexes.

3 Karting and Quad-Biking
Would-be Grand Prix winners can test their skills to the limit at karting circuits at Pafos, Polis, Limassol, Larnaka and Ayia Napa. Quad-bikes can also be hired at Ayia Napa for thrills on the nearby dunes.

4 Horse Riding
There are equestrian centres and country clubs to be found in Nicosia, Limassol and at Pegeia, near Pafos, catering to experienced riders as well as offering lessons and equipment for beginners.

5 Ten-Pin Bowling
The tumbling of skittles can be heard at state-of-the-art air-conditioned bowling centres in Ayia Napa (where there is a combined bowling alley and Internet café on the waterfront), Pafos, Polis, Larnaka and Limassol. Most places are open from noon until 2am.

6 Angling
Cyprus Fisheries Department: Aiolou 13, Nicosia; 22 807 862
Angling is offered year-round from the banks of more than 20 fresh-water reservoirs stocked with trout, largemouth bass, carp, pike-perch and roach. Licences are required and can be obtained from the Cyprus Fisheries Department.

7 Mountain Biking
You don't have to be super-fit to explore Cyprus by mountain bike. Around the resorts there is plenty of fairly flat farmland, and it doesn't take long to find yourself among rolling fields and woodland. With its network of rugged tracks – suitable only for mountain bikes or 4WD vehicles – the Akamas Peninsula

Mountain biking in Cyprus

is ideal territory. Cyprus hosts two annual mountain bike races, the Afxentia International in early spring every year and the Ayia Napa International each November.

8 Golf

MAP B5: Elea Golf Club; Paphos; 26 202 004; www.eleaestate.com ▪ MAP B6: Aphrodite Hills; between Pafos and Limassol; 26 828 200; www.aphroditehills.com ▪ MAP B5: Minthis Hills Golf Club; near Pafos; 26 642 774, www.cyprusgolf.com ▪ MAP B5: Secret Valley Golf Club; 18 km (11 miles) east of Pafos; 26 642 774; www.cyprusgolf.com

Cyprus has perfect golfing weather for much of the year, although some people may find July and August uncomfortably hot. Courses, all 18-hole, include the Faldo-designed Elea, Aphrodite Hills, and the Minthis Hills and Secret Valley Country clubs.

Golf at Aphrodite Hills

9 Skiing

There is skiing on 1,952-m (6,404-ft) Mount Olympus from early January to late March, with ski lifts on the north slope of the mountain and at Sun Valley on the south side.

10 Adrenaline Activities

You don't have to be mad to ascend a shaky, 65-m (213-ft) high tower, then leap from the top attached to a length of elastic cord – but it helps. Ayia Napa, that magnet for youthful thrill-seekers, is Cyprus's bungee capital. Also available are the "skycoaster" and the "slingshot" – which, instead of sending you plummeting towards the ground, fire you into the air.

TOP 10 CYCLING TRAILS

Trail from Akrotiri to the Salt Lake

1 Ayia Napa Promenade
MAP J4
Central Ayia Napa to Agia Thekla and back is 9.5 km (6 miles) on the flat.

2 Around Pafos
MAP A5
Starting by the harbour, take in Pafos's main sights in a 5-km (3-mile) ride.

3 Psilo Dendro Forest
MAP C4
From the Troödos Resort to Caledonia Falls – 13 km (8 miles), all downhill.

4 Troödos Forest
MAP C4
Starting at Psilo Dendro, a shady 10-km (6-mile) run to Kato Amiantos.

5 Troödos to Kryos Potamos
MAP C4
A short but fairly energetic 8 km (5 miles) on wooded slopes.

6 Pyrgos to Governor's Beach
MAP E6
A 13-km (8-mile) downhill run from the Troödos foothills ends at one of the island's better beaches.

7 Lythrodontas-Lefkara
MAP E5
A challenging 14.5-km (9-mile) ride to the pretty lace-makers' village.

8 Akrotiri and the Salt Lake
MAP D6
Look out for flamingoes and pelicans on this 30-km (19-mile) lagoon circuit.

9 Gialias Loop
MAP E4
Mountain breezes take some of the heat out of this 32-km (20-mile) tour, starting and finishing at Lythrodontas.

10 The Akamas Peninsula
MAP A4
This 20-km (12.5-mile) ride from Agios Georgios to Lakki is for tougher riders.

🔟 **Walking Trails**

Stunning views on the Atalanti Trail

① **Atalanti Trail**
MAP C4

A breathtaking panorama rewards walkers on this circular trail, which passes through forests of black pine and centuries-old juniper on its way around the slopes of Mount Olympus, the highest summit of the Troödos massif. Starting and finishing in the square at the centre of the Troödos Resort, the 12-km (7.5-mile) walk takes around four hours.

② **Caledonia Trail**
MAP C5

This is a fairly gentle amble in the woods, from the Presidential Forest Lodge (where Cypriot presidents come to cool off and think things over) to the famous waterfall in its wooded ravine (see p104). Following the course of the aptly named Kryos Potamos ("Cold River") which never dries up and is ideal for cooling hot feet, look out for birds, butterflies and abundant wild flowers in spring and early summer. You can do the walk in less than 90 minutes at an easy pace.

③ **Persephone Trail**
MAP C4

For those who want to work up an appetite before dinner, or burn off calories after lunch, this brisk stroll is ideal. Start just south of Troödos Square in Troödos Resort and walk through lush woods to the Makria Kondarka viewpoint, 1,700 m (5,577 ft) above sea level. The farmlands of the Limassol plain spread out below you.

④ **Profitis Ilias**
MAP J4

Starting at Profitis Ilias church on the Protaras-Paralimni road, this trail leads through hilly fields and pastures, passing the tiny chapels of Agii Saranta and Agios Ioannis and ends up at Konnos Beach.

Konnas Bay, seen from Profitis Ilias

⑤ **Lefkara Circular Trail**
MAP E5

Lefkara, with its old stone cottages, is viewed at its best from above. This uphill short stroll – only 3 km (2 miles) and about 90 minutes there and back – leads from the village's main street to the hilltop chapel of Metamorfosis tou Sotiros (Transfiguration of the Saviour) and views that sweep over Lefkara and the Agios Minas monastery.

⑥ **Horteri Trail**
MAP B4

In the pine-scented heart of Cyprus's largest forest, this is a 5-km (3-mile)

Waterfall on the Caledonia Trail

uphill hike that is best done in spring or autumn, starting and finishing from the Platanouthkia spring outside Stavros tis Psokas.

7 Selladi tou Stavros
MAP B4

A short stroll through the woods around Stavros covers 3 km (2 miles) and allows visits to the Forest Station with its breeding flock of endangered mouflon sheep.

8 Gerakies Trail
MAP C4

This short walk, starting outside Gerakies, covers 3.5 km (2.5 miles) with fine views of the lush Marathasa Valley and the Pafos Forest.

9 Artemis Trail
MAP C4

In spring and autumn, crocuses, cyclamen and anemones greet walkers on this high trail, which meanders off from the Chionistra-Troödos and Troödos-Prodromos road junction and ends in the centre of Troödos village. Look out for the ruins of a 16th-century fort where a handful of Venetians made a gallant last stand against the Ottoman invaders in 1571. This pleasant 8-km (5-mile) walk should take less than three hours.

Anemone

Lighthouse at Cape Gkreko

10 Agii Anargyri
MAP J4

A stiff clifftop walk, starting at the pretty church of Agii Anargyri above Konnos Beach with a detour to Cape Gkreko and its lighthouse.

TOP 10 ANIMALS AND BIRDS

Cyprus mouflon

1 Cyprus Mouflon
Now almost extinct in the wild, this rare native sheep can be seen in sanctuaries.

2 Flamingo
Greater flamingoes spend the winter on salt lakes near Akrotiri and Larnaka.

3 Pelican
Although not native to the island, migrating pelicans are sometimes seen resting on Akrotiri's salt lake.

4 Cyprian Hare
The shy Cyprian hare has been hunted almost to extinction but is sometimes seen by alert walkers.

5 Cyprus Tree Rat
This nut-eating rodent favours a diet of carob beans and almonds.

6 Hoopoe
With its zebra-striped crest of quills and pale pink plumage, the hoopoe is graceful and unmistakable.

7 Rollers and Bee-Eaters
These insect-eating birds, with turquoise, green and yellow plumage, are most often seen in spring.

8 Cranes
Demoiselle and common cranes fly over Cyprus in spring and autumn, en route between their breeding grounds in Asia Minor and their winter homes in Africa.

9 Whip Snake
The inoffensive whip snake, glossy black in colour, flees from people but is sometimes seen wriggling at speed across country roads.

10 Starred Agama
Look for these foot-long mini-dragons, which can be seen scuttling around rocks on the beach or in fields.

🔟 Natural Beauty Spots

1 Akamas Peninsula

A rugged escarpment, covered with juniper and pine trees and fringed by the last of Cyprus's undeveloped beaches, the Akamas Peninsula is the country's only remaining expanse of wilderness. Turtles lay their eggs on its coasts, and its dirt tracks – which are best explored with a four-wheel drive – are a welcome escape from the bustle of the seaside resorts *(see pp32–3)*.

2 Cedar Valley
MAP C4

The towering cedars, with their spreading green boughs, give this valley – high in the Tripylos mountain forest – its name and aromatic scent. They are in the same category as the "cedars of Lebanon" mentioned in the Old Testament and prized by the ship-builders of the ancient world. These trees grow at altitudes between 1,000–2,200 m (3,280–7,218 ft) and are only found here, in the Lebanon, Morocco and southwestern Turkey.

3 Petra tou Romiou
MAP B6

Legend claims that Aphrodite, Greek goddess of love and beauty, was born from the sea-foam just offshore from this pebbly bay, dominated by rugged limestone crags rising from the sea. Other myths say these boulders were hurled at the ships of Saracen corsairs by Digenis Akritas, paladin of the Byzantine frontier.

Limestone crags at Petra tou Romiou

Kelefos bridge in Diarizos Valley

4 Diarizos Valley
MAP C5

Greener and better irrigated than the arid Xeros, the upper Diarizos Valley is studded with medieval churches, farming villages and two arched Venetian bridges, originally built to enable camel- or mule-trains to carry copper ore from mountain mines down to Pafos.

5 Caledonia Falls

A shady refuge from the summer heat, this 11-m (36-ft) waterfall, plunging into a thickly wooded gully, is perhaps named after the *chelidonia* (swallows) which swoop around the falls and pool throughout the summer *(see p104)*.

6 Mount Tripylos
MAP C4

The 1,362-m (4,470-ft) Mount Tripylos is the highest peak in western Cyprus. There are great views over the Tillyrian wilderness to the west and Pafos Forest to the southeast, but it is a harder climb than Mount Olympus.

7 Xeros Valley
MAP B5

The watercourse in this rugged valley often dries up during the summer (*xeros* means dry). However, there is enough water for much of the year for the Venetians to have built a fine bridge across – the Roudias bridge, near Vretsia village. The Xeros eventually feeds the Asprokremmos reservoir, which is a mecca for anglers.

8 Mount Olympos

A jagged and often snow-capped massif, Olympos (also known as Chionistra) shares its name with the home of the gods on the Greek mainland. At 1,952 m (6,404 ft), its highest peak can be seen from all over the island (see p104).

Stunning views from Mount Olympos

9 Salt Lake
MAP D6

This unique wetland is best visited in winter and spring, when its sparkling waters draw large flocks of migrant flamingoes and other waterfowl.

10 Cape Arnaoutis and Baths of Aphrodite
MAP A3

The rugged tip of the Akamas Peninsula is a great place at which to watch the sun plummet into the Mediterranean. Just under 8 km (5 miles) from the cape, a spring, the Baths of Aphrodite, trickles from limestone cliffs into a grotto concealed by fig trees and pink-flowering oleander.

TOP 10 NATIVE FLOWERS

1 Cyclamen
Pink and white Cyprus cyclamen (*Cyclamen cyprium*) flower on sheltered hillsides in autumn.

2 Anemone
Purple, white and red anemones or "wind-flowers" bloom in January.

3 Giant Orchid
Growing up to 1 m (3 ft) high, the giant orchid (*Barlia robertiana*) is spectacular.

4 Narcissus
White and yellow narcissi, relatives of the daffodil, bloom in early spring.

5 Grape Hyacinth
With its bunches of tiny blue globes, the grape hyacinth (*Muscari parviflorum*) is another early spring blossom.

6 Cyprus Tulip
Found only in Cyprus, this dark-red tulip (*Tulipa cypria*) blooms in March or April in the Akamas Peninsula.

7 Lefkara Vetch
Unique to Cyprus, this broad-leafed flower (*Astragalus macrocarpus lefkarensis*) is found only in the wooded hills around Lefkara.

8 Cardoon
With its glossy purple crown and spiky leaves, this regal relative of the humble thistle and the artichoke was valued as a good food source during hard times.

9 Gladiolus
Great swaths of three-leaved gladioli (*Gladiolus triphyllus*) come into vivid flower in early April.

10 Giant Fennel
This towering umbilifer with a greenish-yellow crown is poisonously inedible, but its canes were once used for making furniture.

Cyclamen on a Cyprus hillside

Following pages A rocky outcrop overlooking Cape Gkreko, Ayia Napa

🔟 Children's Attractions

1 Ocean Aquarium, Protaras

MAP J4 ■ Leoforos Protaras ■ Open Apr–Oct: 10am–6pm daily; Nov–Mar: 9am–4pm daily ■ Adm

It may be difficult to tear the kids away from this cool cavern full of tanks housing scary piranhas and sharks, morays, stingrays and hundreds of other inhabitants of the underwater world. It could be even more difficult to persuade them to go back in the water after they have seen what may lurk beneath. In the aquarium gardens, there are also crocodile and turtle ponds and a penguin house.

2 Magic Dancing Waters, Protaras

MAP J4 ■ Leoforos Protaras ■ Shows Apr–Nov: 9pm daily ■ Adm

Children (and most likely parents) will be enthralled by this one-hour display of illuminated fountains that seem to make the water dance and change colour to a programme of classical and pop music themes. Get there early or book in advance from the tourist office, as seats are always at a premium.

3 CitySightseeing, Pafos

MAP A5 ■ Pafos harbour ■ Tours depart 10am–4pm daily ■ Adm (free for under 5s)

This tour, on a bright red open-top bus, covers all the main sights,

including the Fort of Pafos, the harbourside, the Tombs of the Kings, the old town and Agia Kyriaki Church.

4 Mazotos Camel Park

MAP F5 ■ Mazotos ■ Open summer: 9am–7pm daily; winter: 9am–5pm daily ■ Adm

Camels were once the main mode of freight haulage in Cyprus and this park is where they can still be seen. As well as offering camel rides, this family-friendly attraction has a petting zoo, playground and swimming pool.

Mazotos Camel Park

5 Fasouri Watermania, Limassol

Open May–Oct: 10am–6pm daily

Fasouri is the largest of the Cyprus water parks, with more than 30 rides, such as the near-vertical Kamikaze Slide, as well as activities for toddlers *(see p91)*. There are also restaurants, snack bars and a souvenir shop.

Fasouri Watermania, Limassol

Elephants at Pafos Zoo

6 Pafos Zoo
MAP A4 ▪ Pegeia ▪ Open Apr–Oct: 9am–6pm daily (to 7pm Aug); Nov–Mar: 9am–5pm daily ▪ Adm
Camels, mouflon and meerkats are just some of the animals to see at this park near Coral Bay. There is also a collection of exotic birds, all housed in gardens that replicate their natural environments. A restaurant, shop and children's farm are also on the site.

7 WaterWorld, Ayia Napa
Drop to Atlantis and the Fall of Icarus are two of the more adventurous rides for older children and adults at this vast waterpark *(see p16)*. Among the many attractions suitable for younger children are Danaides Waterworks playground, Poseidon's wave pool and the Pegasus Pool.

8 Lemesos Mini Zoo
MAP D6 ▪ Municipal Gardens, Limassol ▪ Open 9am–4pm daily (to 7pm depending on season) ▪ Adm
This recently renovated and well landscaped mini zoo has a spacious aviary with a wide range of exotic birds, as well as ostriches and cheetahs, plus pleasant gardens and a large children's playground. The zoo is located within the town's municipal gardens. The most pleasant way to reach here from the centre of town is by strolling along the seafront promenade, Christodoulou Hatzipavlou.

9 Aphrodite Waterpark, Pafos
MAP A5 ▪ Posidonos, Kato Pafos ▪ Open 10am–5:30pm daily ▪ Adm
Fun for all the family is the theme of this enormous water park, which boasts over 30 rides and attractions, ranging from fairly gentle slides and floats to exciting five-lane "mat racing", a simulated wave pool and a shallow pool for toddlers. The park offers a very welcome break from the often oppressive summer heat.

Yellow Submarine, Ayia Napa

10 Yellow Submarine, Ayia Napa
MAP J4 ▪ Ayia Napa Harbour ▪ Departures 10:30am, 12:15pm and 2:30pm daily ▪ Adm (free for children)
See the marine world through the portholes of this miniature 30-seat submarine, which cruises the Ayia Napa coast and its underwater grottoes. The highlights of the cruise include the guided swim through sea caves, and the feeding session, where the skipper attracts fish to eat food from his fingers.

TOP10 Cypriot Dishes

Traditional Greek Cypriot *afelia*

1 Afelia
Lean cubes of tender pork, marinated overnight in red wine and flavoured with cumin, cinnamon, coriander and pepper, is the main ingredient of this quintessentially Greek Cypriot casserole dish.

2 Meze
Meze is the keynote of Cypriot cooking – not a single dish, but a massive medley of samples including delicious dips, tasty prawns, whitebait, squid and other fish, charcuterie or hot sausages, grilled cheese, and raw or cooked vegetables that are in season. It's all accompanied by local wine, beer or *zivania* (distilled spirit).

3 Souvla
The simplest and most delicious of Cypriot dishes, *souvla* is made with chunks of pork, goat or lamb, skewered and grilled over charcoal, then served with French fries

Souvla

and a salad of lettuce or cabbage, tomatoes, onions and pickled hot peppers.

4 Pittes
Pittes (turnovers) are a popular snack in Cyprus and are easily available in any good bakery. They can be both sweet and savoury in taste, depending on the ingredient used as filling. Favourite varieties include *eliopitta* (olive turnover), *tashinopitta* (stuffed with sesame paste) and *kolokotes* – little triangles filled with pumpkin, cracked wheat and raisins.

Oven-baked *moussaka*

5 Moussakas
Cypriots and Greeks both claim to have invented this filling, oven-cooked casserole, although the name is Arabic. *Moussakas* are often the home-cooked main dish at family occasions such as weddings, christenings and saint's days, and every Cypriot cook has his or her own recipe. The basic ingredients are minced lamb or beef cooked with herbs, red wine and spices and layered between slices of aubergine (eggplant), then covered with a white béchamel sauce and baked in the oven.

6 Sheftalia
These tasty mini-burgers made with minced pork and aromatic herbs often appear as part of a *meze* array or as an appetizer, but

are equally good as a main course, when they are usually served with salad and the inevitable French fries.

7 Louvi me Lahana

This bean salad is a hearty, meat-free option for vegetarians, and is made using cold, cooked black-eye beans mixed with plenty of green leafy vegetables – the exact mix depends on the time of year – dressed with olive oil and plenty of freshly squeezed lemon juice.

8 Koupepia

Cypriots say this dish, made with vine leaves stuffed with minced pork or lamb and rice, is at its best in spring when the young leaves are at their freshest and most tender. When *koupepia* are made in winter, cabbage leaves are sometimes used as a substitute for this reason.

9 Melintzanes Yiahni

On the Turkish side of the "Attila Line", this mélange of aubergines baked in oil, with a delicious sauce of garlic and fresh tomatoes, is called *imam bayildi*. In either language, it is one of the tastiest vegetarian options that Cyprus has to offer.

Classic *ofto kleftiko*

10 Ofto Kleftiko

This hearty dish is lamb baked in a domed outdoor oven in its own juices, with herbs and spices, until it is so tender that it falls off the bone. Often served with baked vegetables, it is a good choice for cooler weather.

TOP 10 MEZE DISHES

Grilled halloumi cheese

1 Tahini
Sesame seeds are the key ingredient of this dip, ground with garlic, lemon juice, olive oil and cumin, and garnished with flat-leafed parsley.

2 Agrellia Wild Asparagus
A strictly springtime treat, this dish comes in light and dark variants and is often served with scrambled eggs.

3 Karaoli Yahni
Tiny wild snails are a prized Greek Cypriot delicacy. In this dish they are served stewed in tomato sauce.

4 Zalatina
Zalatina, or brawn, is usually served with a relish of capers and a wild spiny pickle called *kapari*.

5 Moungra
Pickled cauliflower is another *meze* favourite to accompany meat snacks, especially during the winter and Lent.

6 Ochtapodi Krasato
A seafood favourite, chunks of octopus are marinated and then simmered slowly in red wine that is spiced with cumin and coriander.

7 Barbouni
These tiny red mullet are bony but delicious when served fried.

8 Halloumi Cheese
Grilled halloumi cheese has a chewy texture and is strongly flavoured.

9 Lountza
Lean pork tenderloin traditionally smoked with *lentisc* (mastic) leaves and branches is another must-try *meze* option.

10 Bourekia
If you can find room for dessert, these tiny pastries stuffed with *anari* cheese and doused in honey are delicious.

🔟 Wineries and Breweries

Vineyard in the Troödos foothills

① Vouni Panayia Winery
MAP C5 ■ Vouni ■ 26 722 770
■ Open 8am–5:30pm daily

Taking advantage of Panagia's perfect soil and climate is the Vouni Panayia winery, which produces the good dry white Alina, hefty red Plakota and fine Pampela rosé, all of which can be tasted and bought here.

② Tsangarides
MAP B5 ■ Lemona village
■ 26 722 777 ■ Open 9am–5pm Mon–Sat

Established in 2004, Tsangarides is an excellent family-run winery that produces wines organically in a privileged microclimate. Their signature labels include Shiraz rosé, Mataro red and Xynisteri dry white, all of which are made from either imported or native grapes. They are available at Pafos tavernas.

③ Vlassides Winery
MAP C5 ■ Kilani ■ 99 441 574
■ Open 8am–4pm Mon–Sat

This state-of-the-art microwinery offers high-quality reds, whites and rosés prepared from imported and local grape varieties, both blended and unblended. Sample their premium red, oak-aged private collection or Sauvignon Blanc white.

④ Kamanterena
MAP B4 ■ Kato Stroumbi, near Polemi ■ 26 633 000 ■ Tastings 8am–3pm Mon–Fri

Formerly the undistinguished, mass-market SODAP winery, Kamanterena has come a long way and established itself as an international award-winner, particularly for its Xynisteri dry white and St Barnabas Commandaria.

⑤ Tsiakkas Winery
MAP D5 ■ Pitsilias, near Pelendri ■ 25 991 080 ■ Open 9am–5pm daily

Located high in the Limassol foothills, Tsiakkas produces a wide range of red, white and rosé wines, both from imported and native grape varieties. Go for their award-winning oak-aged Cabernet red.

A tasting at the Tsiakkas Winery

Gaia Oinotechniki

MAP C5 ■ Archiepiskopou Makariou 25, Agios Ambrosios ■ 25 943 981 ■ Open 8am–3pm Mon–Fri

Out of the five wine varieties produced here, three are certified organic. Their Salome red and Oenanthi rosé wines have been around since the early 1990s.

7 Monte Royia

MAP B4 ■ 26 722 455 ■ Shop: Open 10am–6pm daily

The monks of Chrysorrogiatissa monastery *(see p41)* grow their own grapes on the hillsides around Panagia and produce an excellent dry white Agios Andronikos.

Aphrodite's Rock Brewing Company

8 Aphrodite's Rock Brewing Company

MAP B5 ■ Polis Road, Tsada ■ 26 101 466 ■ Open 11:30am–10pm Mon–Sat, noon–5pm Sun

The first craft brewery in Cyprus is British-run and offers tasting and sales of a half-dozen ales, bitters, lagers and porter.

9 Nelion Winery

MAP C5 ■ Pretori village ■ 25 442 445 ■ Open 9am–6pm daily

The leading winery of the Diarizos Valley, Nelion prepares half a dozen labels of dry and medium dry wines.

 Fikardos

MAP B5 ■ Mesogi Industrial Estate ■ 26 949 814 ■ Open 8am–1pm & 2–5pm Mon–Fri, 8am–1pm Sat

The oldest private winery in Pafos, Fikardos' best labels are the crisp Xinisteri-Semillon Amalthia white and the dry Mataro rosé.

TOP 10 DRINKS

Cypriot wines

1 Ouzo
Sweet and aniseed flavoured, ouzo has its roots in Greece. It turns milky white when water is added.

2 Zivania
Similar to French marc or Italian grappa, this drink is traditionally consumed with nuts, dried fruits or a full *meze*.

3 Brandy
Drunk on its own or in a variety of cocktails. Brandy Sour is the classic Cypriot cocktail and very palatable.

4 Wine
Red, rosé and white local wines are generally unpretentious, quaffable and cheap, and quality continues to improve.

5 Filfar
This sticky-sweet liqueur, distilled from oranges or lemons is supposedly taken from a Venetian recipe.

6 Mosphilo
Unique to Cyprus, *mosphilo* is a sweet-sour liqueur distilled from the red berries of the hawthorn tree.

7 Beers
The only surviving mass-market beers in Cyprus are KEO, Leon and Carlsberg. Most foreign beers are also available everywhere.

8 Coffee
Starbucks and Costa Coffee are here, but you should also try *ellinikos kafes*, served in a tiny cup with a large amount of sugar and sediment.

9 Cocktails
From the Brandy Sour to the saucy Sex on the Beach, Cypriot bars offer extensive cocktail lists.

10 Spring Water
Water bottled from the Troödos and the Akamas springs is widely available.

🔟 Cyprus For Free

The "Green Line" runs through the divided city of Nicosia

1 Walk the "Green Line"
Stroll along Nicosia's "Green Line" *(see p72)* with its abandoned houses, graffiti and UN and Greek Cypriot bunkers. Look out for the Selimiye Mosque minaret with its Turkish flag as you head for Ermou Street, which originally bisected the Old City and now buzzes with galleries, artists' studios and music venues.

2 Festivals
The Cypriot calendar includes plenty of free annual festivals and traditional celebrations; August is a popular month for these carnival-like village festivals *(see pp66–7)*.

3 Free Tours
The Cyprus Tourism Organization in Nicosia *(see p122)* offer two free guided tours weekly, leaving at 10am from the tourist office and lasting 2 hours and 45 minutes.

4 Contemporary Art
MAP P3 ▪ State Gallery of Contemporary Art, cnr Stasinou & Kritis, Nicosia ▪ 22 458 228 ▪ Open 10am–5pm Mon–Fri, 10am–1pm Sat ▪ Closed Aug
This excellent art gallery showcases some of the finest Cypriot artists and sculptors from the 20th century in galleries spread over three floors.

5 Coastal Walk
A partially paved coastal path stretches 5 km (3 miles) from the headland in Pafos towards Coral Bay. It passes meadows of wild flowers, pristine sandy beaches and has strategically located benches for contemplating the sea views.

6 Archaeological Sites
From spooky catacombs and ancient tombs to the remains of a magnificent 4th-century basilica, several of Pafos's ancient sites are free to visit *(see p92)*. They include the Agia Solomoni and Christian catacombs, Agios Lambrianos Rock-Cut Tomb, St Paul's Pillar and the fascinating Agia Kyriaki Basilica.

7 Monasteries and Churches
Virtually all of Cyprus's magnificent monasteries and churches are free

Chrysopolitissa Church, Pafos

to visit, and combine superbly preserved architecture with priceless frescoes, icons, and artwork. Several of the most impressive are located in the Troödos Mountains, including Agios Ioannis Lambadistis and Kykkos Monastery. Agios Mamas in Louvaras *(see p74)* is also worth visiting.

8 Markets
MAP P2 & A5 respectively
■ **Büyük Han, North Nicosia; Ktima Pafos Bazaar**

The meticulously restored Ottoman Büyük Han houses a number of shops offering local crafts. The upper Pafos market is more authentic, featuring antique stalls.

Market stalls selling local crafts

9 Cultural Centres
MAP P3 ■ **British Council, Aristotelous 1–3, Old Town, Nicosia** ■ **9–11am Mon–Thu (also 3:30–5:30pm Tue & Wed)**

The British Council offers a well-stocked, limited-hours library where you can sift through books about Cyprus in English.

10 Views of Varosia
MAP J4 ■ **Cultural Centre of Occupied Famagusta, Evagorou 35, Deryneia** ■ **7:30am–4:30pm Mon–Fri, 9:30am–4:30pm Sat**

Varosia, a former booming seaside resort, has been a ghost town since the Turkish invasion of 1974.

TOP MONEY SAVING TIPS

Local produce at Limassol market

1 Visit Cyprus off-season to be sure of getting the best deals; in particular avoid school holidays, Christmas, western Easter and the Greek Orthodox Easter season (dates vary annually).

2 Students, teachers and senior citizens are entitled to reduced admission at many museums, as long as they can show proof of status.

3 Staying in a self-catering apartment can offer major savings, especially for families. Buy food, drinks and snacks at local shops and markets.

4 When eating out, order Cypriot bottled wines rather than expensive, imported wines. The best Cypriot labels compare in quality with French or Greek wines that usually feature on the wine lists.

5 Shop locally for picnic ingredients to take to the beach or a designated picnic ground.

6 Local tourist offices can provide a calendar of free events taking place nearby, from village festivals and religious processions to cultural events and musical performances.

7 Pack a carry-on bag carefully and take advantage of low, no-checked-luggage airfares to Cyprus.

8 It is usually possible to find holiday work in high season, especially in bars, clubs and restaurants. However, hours tend to be long and pay low, and working conditions less than perfect.

9 Hitchhiking is permitted and Cypriots tend to be quite generous in offering free rides, at least in remote areas.

10 Dine at a *mageireio* (cook house) – popular, inexpensive Cypriot restaurants that specialize in home-style stews.

TOP 10 Cultural and Traditional Festivals

1 Carnival, Limassol
Feb–Mar

Limassol comes to life during the 10 days before Lent, when islanders indulge themselves with feasts and fancy-dress parades. Carnival is also celebrated elsewhere on the island, but Limassol's celebrations are traditionally the liveliest and most entertaining.

Carnival parade, Limassol

2 International Bellapais Music Festival
May–Jun

This superb annual festival is held at Bellapais Abbey in Kyrenia. Up to nine classical concerts and recitals are held, featuring world-class musicians and performers.

3 Kourion Summer Events
Jun–Jul

Kourion's amphitheatre with its magnificent hillside location *(see pp26–7)* makes the perfect venue for staging a Shakespeare play, usually during the third week of June. In July, the same amphitheatre hosts music concerts by leading Greek stars.

4 Larnaka Festival
Jul

Larnaka takes its place in the limelight when musicians, dancers and actors – many of them from Greece, Balkan and eastern European countries and the former Soviet Union – arrive here to perform at the various ancient, medieval and early 20th-century venues spread all over the city.

5 International Pharos Chamber Music Festival, Kouklia
May–Jun

Organised by the Pharos Foundation, this popular music festival features performances by up-and-coming and established artists at the UNESCO-listed, medieval Royal Manor House at Kouklia in Palaipafos (Old Pafos). The Pharos Foundation also hosts similar events at The Shoe Factory in Nicosia.

6 International Festival of Ancient Greek Drama, Pafos
Jul–Aug

The works of ancient playwrights such as Sophocles, Euripides and Aristophanes leap back to life in Pafos's ancient odeon during this internationally renowned cultural event. It attracts performers and directors from Cyprus, Greece and further afield.

7 Commandaria Festival
Jul

Wine flows freely and there is dancing in the streets as Kouris Valley's vineyard villages – Alassa, Agios Georgios, Doros, Lania, Monagri and Silikou – celebrate the start of the grape harvest, some of which goes in the making of commandaria – the heavy Cypriot dessert wine.

8 Pafos Aphrodite Opera Festival

Sep

A month after the Greek drama festival, the area in front of Pafos castle comes alive again as the setting for three days of opera during the first week of the month, performed by an esteemed international cast. This is one of the highlights of the country's cultural calendar.

9 Limassol Wine Festival

Aug–Sep

This is the perfect time to sample Cyprus's dozens of wines in depth, at length and, best of all, for free. Limassol's wine-makers celebrate the harvest by sponsoring 10 days of wine tastings, held in the city's attractive municipal gardens. The whole event is accompanied with outdoor live music and dancing in the evenings.

Ayia Napa International Festival

10 Ayia Napa International Festival

Sep

Three nights towards the end of the month witness free concerts in Ayia Napa's central plaza by Cypriot musicians and renowned Greek stars. There are also folk dance performances by international groups.

Pafos Aphrodite Opera Festival

TOP 10 ORTHODOX RELIGIOUS FESTIVALS

Lighting tapers on Easter Sunday

1 Agios Vassilios
On St Basil's Eve islanders have a meal which culminates with *vasilopitta*, a sweet loaf containing a coin that brings good luck to its finder. *31 Dec & 1 Jan*

2 Ta Fota (Epiphany)
In harbour towns youths vie for the honour of retrieving a crucifix thrown into the sea. *6 Jan*

3 Green Monday
Across the island, families take this day off to fly kites and grill meat in conspicuous violation of Lent, and as a gesture against the Church. *Feb–Mar*

4 Evangelismos (Annunciation)
The Annunciation is celebrated as a Greek national holiday. *25 Mar*

5 Good Friday
Christ's funeral bier, decorated with flowers, is carried solemnly through the streets by each parish at nightfall. *Apr or May*

6 Easter Saturday
After midnight mass, villagers take home a taper lit from a blessed candle. *Apr or May*

7 Easter Sunday
Villagers roast a goat and town-dwellers head to grill restaurants. *Apr or May*

8 Kataklysmos
Noah's escape from the Flood is celebrated with processions and music in coastal towns. *May or Jun*

9 Dormition of the Virgin
The "Falling Asleep" of Mary is marked by pilgrimages to the island's churches bearing the name of the Virgin. *15 Aug*

10 Christmas
Christmas is a low-key affair, confined mostly to family gatherings. *25 Dec*

Cyprus
Area by Area

Harbour at Kyrenia, Northern Cyprus

TOP 10 Central Cyprus

The heartland of Cyprus is full of variety, from the bustle of Nicosia, the island's capital, to old-fashioned villages and age-old churches in the foothills of the Troödos mountain range. This is a part of Cyprus that remains unexplored by many visitors, yet it warrants investigation. It is the best place to see the true face of the island – Nicosia is far less absorbed in tourism than the coastal resorts and the same is true of outlying villages. The walled city has an atmosphere all of its own, with sleepy, sunbaked streets and authentic cafés, and the opportunity to experience the reality of the divided city first-hand by crossing over to the Turkish-occupied north for a day.

Ivory throne, Cyprus Museum

1 Strovolos

MAP F3 ■ Pancyprian **Geographical Museum:** Leoforos Strovolou 100; 22 470 340; Open 9am–3:30pm Mon–Fri (to 5pm Wed), 9am–1pm Sat; Adm

The unique Pancyprian Geographical Museum – the only one of its kind in Cyprus – within an attractively restored traditional building is the main reason for visiting Strovolos. It is dedicated to the island's natural history, with displays of minerals, especially copper, which made Cyprus wealthy in pre-Christian

times, and Cypriot fauna and old maps. The town itself is built around the 18th-century church of Agios Georgios (one of several churches named after St George in this part of Cyprus), and is now essentially a suburb of Nicosia.

2 Nicosia Walled City

Cyprus's capital city is a mélange of medieval, colonial and modern influences. Within the brooding ramparts built by the Venetians are the narrow streets and pretty restored buildings of the Laiki

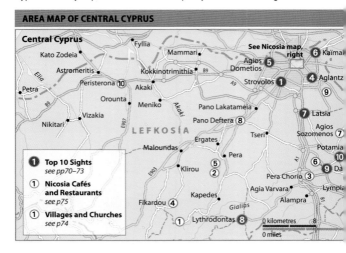

AREA MAP OF CENTRAL CYPRUS

The Nicosia cityscape

Geitonia pedestrianized district, which is full of souvenir shops and cafés. But the city also offers many museums and heritage sites celebrating every aspect of Nicosia's history, from its ancient past to its traditional crafts (see pp12–13).

3 Cyprus Museum

A treasury of archaeological finds here, from sites all over Cyprus, wonderfully illustrate the island's historic past and make this the most fascinating of its museums. Exhibits highlight the skills of sculptors, metalworkers, potters, painters and other craftsmen across more than four millennia (see pp14–15).

4 Aglantzia
MAP F3

Not so very long ago, Aglantzia, which dates back as far as 3888 BC, was a vibrant village community in its own right, thriving on agriculture, stockbreeding and quarrying. Today, although it has virtually become a suburb of Nicosia, it still retains a village ambience, with hilly streets, numerous parks and a handful of pretty 18th-century churches. Among these is the one-domed, arch-roofed Agios Georgios church, which contains a woodcut iconostasis decorated with images of baskets and flowers.

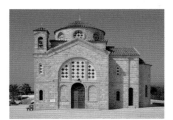

Aglantzia's Agios Georgios church

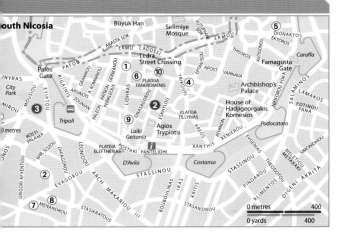

5 Agios Dometios
MAP F3

The pretty, late 17th-century church of Agios Dometios is the focus of this village community. Although it's on the outskirts of the capital, Agios Dometios still moves at its own leisurely pace, and it's a nice spot to stop for a cup of coffee or a cold drink.

Church of Agios Dometios

6 Kaïmakli
MAP F3 ■ Open daily
■ Dis. access

Two pretty churches are the jewels of this village. Although they are not that old by Cypriot standards – the Church of the Archangel dates from the 18th century and the church of Agia Varvara is a mere late 19th-century addition – they are worth visiting nonetheless for the excess of ornate carving, silver-framed icons and votive candles that are so typical of the Orthodox faith.

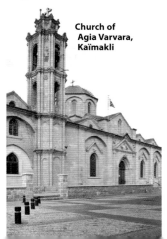

Church of Agia Varvara, Kaïmakli

THE "GREEN LINE"

The "Green Line", also known as Attila Line, **(above)** divides both Cyprus and the city of Nicosia in two and marks the southern extent of the Turkish army's advance in 1974. Stretches of barbed wire, metal fence and sandbags, and a no-man's-land of derelict homes and shops, separate the two halves of Nicosia. Foreign visitors and Greek and Turkish Cypriots may cross the border at any of seven crossing points. The pedestrian crossings are at Ledra Street and Ledra Palace Hotel. Crossings for car or taxis are at Agios Dometios, Pergamos, Agios Nikolaos, Limnitis-Yeşilırmak and Astromeritis-Zodia. You will be issued with a visa on the Turkish side and given permission to stay up to 90 days in Northern Cyprus.

7 Latsia
MAP F4

Plunging through rugged scenery, the Kakarista Gorge at Latsia is this hillside village's most important landmark. It can be explored alone, or with a local guide. Incongruously but entertainingly, the nearby Carlsberg Brewery, just outside the village, is open for visits and houses the Photos Photiades Foundation's Natural History Museum, an exotic repository of stuffed, fossilized and pickled snakes, birds, mammals and marine creatures.

8 Lythrodontas
MAP E4

Located some 25 km (15 miles) south of Nicosia, this village is best known for its olive groves (Lythrodontas claims to have more olive trees than any other village in Cyprus) and "Avli", a beautifully restored complex of traditional buildings offering accommodation. The abandoned Monastery of Prophitis Elias is also worth a visit, and can be found just beyond the village, where the paved road ends.

9 **Dali**

MAP F4

A lively farming village that is little more than a main street lined with shops, traditional cafés and a village church, Dali offers a taste of Cypriot life largely untainted by tourism. It takes its name from one of Cyprus's most ancient city states, Idalion, which archaeologists are continuing to explore nearby (see p74).

Ruins of a church at Agios Sozomenos

10 **Potamia**

MAP F4

If you want to see the effects of the division of the island on a rural community, Potamia is a good place to start. Until 1974, it was roughly half Greek, half Turkish Cypriot, but today only a handful of Turkish Cypriots remain, while exiled Greek Cypriots now live in the properties abandoned by those who left. At the abandoned hamlet of Agios Sozomenos, near Potamia, stands the ruins of Agios Mamas, a triple-apsed, early 16th-century church built in Lusignan style.

A MORNING SHOPPING IN NICOSIA

Start your day at the top of **Stasikratous** and window-shop your way south past ranks of designer stores, then double back along busy **Archiepiskopou Makariou III**. Stop for a cold drink at one of the street's hip cafés.

Cross **Plateia Eleftherias** and enter **Laïki Geitonia** (see p13). This area has been restored as a sanitized version of an old-fashioned Nicosia neighbourhood. You'll find souvenirs aplenty here – some authentic and some trashy. The **Diachroniki Gallery** (Arsinois 84) is a good place to seek out original and facsimile prints and engravings. Nearby, at Ippokratous 2, you can find copies of Byzantine silverware at the **Leventis Museum** gift shop.

Nicosia's main shopping street, **Lidhras**, runs north from Plaeteia Eleftherias. If you're in need of a refreshment, stop into one of the many cafés or ice cream parlours that line this road. If you continue north you can cross the border here into **North Nicosia**, where the shopping street turns into a typical Middle Eastern market.

On the Greek side of the border, head for **Plateia Faneromenis** which is now a bustling arty area dotted with a number of cafés, bars and small shops selling arts and crafts.

If all this food has made you hungry, enjoy lunch at one of the several tavernas that line Lidhras, or its parallel **Onasagorou**.

See map on pp70–71

Villages and Churches

1 Machairas Monastery
MAP E4

This monastery was founded in 1148 by two hermits who discovered an icon of the Virgin, painted by Luke the Evangelist. The icon survived fires which damaged the monastery in 1530 and 1892 – proof, to believers, of its miraculous powers (see p40).

The historic Machairas Monastery

2 Agios Irakleidios Convent
MAP E4 ■ Open 9am–noon, 3–5:30pm daily

One of the oldest Christian communities in Cyprus, the chapel here dates from the 15th century. It lay in ruins before being restored in the 1960s.

3 Pera Chorio
MAP F4

Shepherds, angels and newborn Jesus being bathed are among the most intact 12th-century wall paintings inside Agioi Apostoloi church in this village near Dali.

4 Fikardou
MAP E4

The hill village of Fikardou has won awards for its living museum, which shows Cyprus village life as it was until just decades ago (see p42).

The hillside village of Fikardou

5 Tamassos
MAP E4 ■ Open Apr–Sep: 9:30am–5pm Mon–Fri; Oct–Mar: 8:30am–4pm Mon–Fri ■ Adm

One of the earliest cities on the island (7th century BC), Tamassos grew wealthy from its copper mines, which were famous in the ancient world.

6 Ancient Idalion
MAP F4 ■ Museum: open 8:30am–4pm Mon–Fri; Adm

Dali takes its name from the city-state of Idalion. Adonis was killed by a boar of Idalion and the red flowers that bloom here are deemed tokens of his death. The site is closed for excavation, but the museum exhibits its rich finds.

7 Agios Sozomenos
MAP F4

This deserted village close to the "Green Line" is home to the remains of Agios Mamas, a large Gothic church.

8 Panagia Chrysospiliotissa Church
MAP E4 ■ Deftera ■ Open dawn–dusk daily

Catacombs dug into the hillside show this church dates from early Christian times, when believers worshipped in secret for fear of persecution.

9 La Cava Castle
MAP F3 ■ Closed to the public

Toppled ramparts mark the site of this 14th-century Lusignan keep.

10 Peristerona
MAP D3

This 10th-century church has wall paintings dating from the 12th and 15th centuries.

Nicosia Cafés and Restaurants

PRICE CATEGORIES

For a three-course meal for one with half a bottle of wine (or equivalent meal), taxes and extra charges.

€ under €25 €€ €25–€50 €€€ over €50

(1) Kath'Odon
MAP P2 ▪ Lidhras 62
▪ 22 661 656 ▪ €

Very close to the "Green Line", this lively eatery is one of the most consistent tavernas on Lidhras, featuring a meat-strong menu. Dinner is often accompanied by live music.

Meze dish of grilled halloumi cheese

(2) Pantopoleio Kali Orexi
MAP N3 ▪ Vasileos Pavlou 7
▪ 22 675 151 ▪ €€

Try Greek cuisine with a Cypriot twist at this popular restaurant near Cyprus Museum. Go for squash quiche with mint and cheese or meatballs laced with Chios mastic.

(3) Syrian Arab Friendship Club
Vasilisis Amalias 17, Agios Dometios
▪ 22 776 246 ▪ €

Start your meal with Middle Eastern *meze* and finish it off with Cypriot desserts. Lovely garden seating.

(4) Zanettos
MAP P2 ▪ Trikoupi 65, near
Ömeriye Mosque ▪ 22 765 501 ▪ €

Visit this 1938-founded place for the best *meze* in the old town. Expect snails, liver slices, bean dishes and generous desserts.

(5) Inga's Veggie Heaven
MAP Q2 ▪ Dionaktos 2 ▪ 22 344 674 ▪ Dis. access ▪ €

This superb vegetarian restaurant is run by an Icelandic chef who offers several choices daily, including such dishes as lentil burgers and stuffed peppers. It is set on a small square lined with arts and crafts studios.

(6) Kala Kathoumena
MAP P2 ▪ Nikokleous 19–21
▪ 22 664 654 ▪ Dis. access ▪ €

One of the best trendy cafés in the Fanouromeni area, Kala Kathoumena is a good option for enjoying Cypriot coffee, herbal tea or spoon sweets at good-value prices.

(7) Barrique Wine Deli
MAP N3 ▪ Menandrou 4
▪ 22 663 777 ▪ €€

Originally just a wine shop and deli, this place now offers appetizing light meals such as stuffed mushrooms, smoked duck salad, pasta and cheese-and-charcuterie platters.

(8) Pyxida
MAP N3 ▪ Menandrou 5
▪ 22 445 636 ▪ €€€

Come here for the best seafood in central Nicosia and choose from an array of farmed and frozen fish varieties. There is also an oyster bar next door.

(9) Avo
MAP P3 ▪ Onasagorou, corner Apollonos ▪ 22 661 172 ▪ €

This is the go-to place for the old town's most interesting fast food item – *lahmatzoun*, an Armenian-style pizza served straight from the oven.

(10) Mattheos
MAP P2 ▪ Platela 28 Oktovriou
▪ 22 755 846 ▪ Closed Sun ▪ €

A popular lunch-only *mageireio* set next to Araplar Mosque, Mattheos excels in home-style dishes such as quail, *koupepia*, rabbit, octopus and artichoke with beans.

See map on pp70–71

🔟 Southeast Cyprus

Legendary nightlife and beaches are what draw most visitors to Cyprus's southern and eastern shores each summer, and many people get no further than Ayia Napa or Protaras, or the historic city and bustling port of Larnaka. Yet there is much more to see in this fascinating region: Byzantine churches with age-old icons and frescoes; remarkable Stone Age settlements; and, tucked away in hidden valleys, quaint villages where you can shop for traditional crafts or sit at a pavement café and watch the slow pace of life go by.

Sandy beaches at Protaras

AREA MAP OF SOUTHEAST CYPRUS

1 Protaras
MAP J4

On the east coast, 9 km (5.5 miles) from Ayia Napa, Protaras has grown around a clutch of sandy beaches where the warm, shallow water is a vivid turquoise. At night, Protaras comes into its cosmopolitan own, with a main street lined with bars, cafés and restaurants to suit all tastes. There are plenty of excursions to be made to nearby sights and attractions, such as Fig Tree Bay (see p81).

Flumes at Waterworld Waterpark

2 Chapelle Royale
MAP F5 ▪ Pyrga ▪ Open daily on request ▪ Adm

This little village chapel, dedicated to St Catherine, was built by King Janus and his queen, Charlotte de Bourbon, in 1421. Ask the custodian to let you in to see the colourful remnants of some unique frescoes.

3 Angeloktisti Church
MAP G5 ▪ Kiti village ▪ Open 9am–4:30pm daily ▪ Donation

The star attraction in this historic, 11th-century church is the apsidal mosaic from its 6th-century predecessor. Here the Virgin balances infant Jesus on her left arm, flanked by angels Gabriel on her right and Michael on the left.

- **1** **Top 10 Sights**
  see pp77–79
- **1** **Restaurants**
  see p85
- **1** **The Best of the Rest**
  see p80
- **1** **Beaches**
  see p81
- **1** **Cafés and Eateries**
  see p84
- **1** **Bars and Pubs**
  see p82
- **1** **Nightspots**
  see p83

Larnaka's medieval Fort

4 Larnaka Fort and District Medieval Museum

MAP M6 ▪ South end, Finikoudes Promenade, Larnaka ▪ 24 322 710 ▪ Open 8am–5pm Mon–Fri (to 7:30pm Apr–Sep), 9:30am–5pm Sat & Sun ▪ Adm

Huge rusting cannons stand guard over the waterfront from the battlements of Larnaka's medieval fort, from which there are good views of the bay. Inside, the museum has a gallery on the first floor, with swords and daggers, medieval armour and flintlock muskets outshining an assortment of 12th- to 18th-century pottery and displays of Byzantine, Lusignan and Ottoman odds and ends. Occasionally in summer, open-air theatrical or musical performances are staged here.

5 Pierides Museum, Larnaka

The museum's most notable exhibits include a huge collection of Roman glasses and other relics, such as a 5,000-year old terracotta statue, plus red-and-black bowls and vases and terracotta figures excavated from all over the country. It also displays old embroidery, lace and silver jewellery, along with Cyprus's largest collection of antiquarian maps *(see pp18–19)*.

6 Larnaka Archaeological Museum

MAP L4 ▪ Plateia Kalograion ▪ 24 304 169 ▪ Open 8am–3pm Tue–Fri (to 5pm Thu), 9am–3pm Sat ▪ Adm

Carved limestone column drums and capitals from ancient sites stand in the garden of this museum. Inside is one of the best introductions to the southeast's archaeological sites, with its displays of Stone Age, Bronze Age and Roman discoveries brought here from Choirokoitia, Kalavasos and other local excavations *(see p39)*.

7 Ayia Napa

Ayia Napa, on the south shore of a peninsula that juts towards Cyprus's southeast tip, has risen to fame as one of the world's great dance party destinations, but there is more than mere nightlife to this purpose-built resort. Ayia Napa's core is its main square, which is packed with bars and café tables. Yet, only steps away from the crowds is a tranquil oasis, the medieval Ayia Napa Monastery, while down on the seafront the Limanaki ("little harbour") still has some of its village character, even if, these days, the

Ayia Napa rock arch

fishing boats are outnumbered by pleasure craft carrying holidaymakers to outlying beaches *(see pp16–17)*.

8 Lefkara
MAP E5 ▪ Museum: open Apr–Sep: 9:30am–5pm daily; Oct–Mar: 8:30am–4pm daily; Adm

Famed for its lace-making and silver-smith craftsmanship, Lefkara is home to a multitude of craft shops selling lace, embroidery and jewellery. If you're not in the mood to buy, you can marvel instead at the beautifully made treasures in the small but comprehensive Museum of Traditional Embroidery and Silversmithing.

Ceiling at Stavrovouni Monastery

9 Stavrovouni Monastery
MAP F5 ▪ Open Sep–Mar: 7–11am, 2–5pm daily; Apr–Aug: 7am–noon, 3–7pm daily

This impressive monastery is poised high above the coastal plains on a 750-m (2,444-ft) crag in the foothills of the Troödos range *(see p40)*. Home to a community of 20 monks, it claims to have a fragment of the True Cross. Women cannot enter.

10 Choirokoitia Neolithic Settlement
MAP F5 ▪ Open Apr–Sep: 8:30am–7:30pm daily; Oct–Mar: 8:30am–5pm daily ▪ Adm

Archaeologists believe these are the foundations of a settlement that thrived on this hilltop almost 9,000 years ago. A UNESCO World Heritage Site, some of the round stone houses have been reconstructed.

A HALF-DAY WALK FROM AYIA NAPA TO PROTARAS

▶ This 12-km (7.5-mile) walk, taking about three or four hours (allowing time for swimming stops) is an ideal way to burn off a night's excesses. But for the less energetic, Ayia Napa has plenty of bicycle rental shops. An asphalted bike trail leads round the headland that separates the two resorts. Take plenty of water and wear high-factor sunblock, especially between June and September.

Starting the walk at **Ayia Napa's** harbour, head east along the coast, past **Limanaki** and **Kryo Nero** beaches *(see p81)*. As you leave the last of Ayia Napa's resort hotels behind, the coast becomes progressively rockier, towards the rugged headland of **Cape Gkreko** *(see p17)* and its landmark radar masts. **Kermia** beach, 4 km (2.5 miles) east of Ayia Napa, is a good place to stop for a dip before setting off across country.

The route now skirts the misleadingly named **Ayia Napa Forest**, which is actually an area of native juniper scrub, then passes the scant remnants of a temple to Aphrodite before plunging down to the blue water and pebbles of tiny **Konnos Bay** *(see p81)*, overlooked by the little white **Church of Anargyroi**.

After a refreshing swim in Konnos Bay, you can head back into resort territory before reaching **Protaras** *(see p77)* for a well-earned cold drink. You will find plenty of taxis here that can take you back to **Ayia Napa**. Or opt for public buses 101 and 102.

See map on pp76–7 ←

The Best of the Rest

① Kition

MAP G5 ■ **Archiepiskopou Kyprianou, Chrysopolitissa district, Larnaka** ■ **Open summer: 9:30am–5pm Mon–Fri; winter: 8:30am–4pm Mon–Fri** ■ **Adm**

Foundations of Mycenaean temples dating from the 13th century BC hint at a lost city beneath Larnaka's streets. There are remnants of ancient temples, sacrificial altars and a coppersmith's workshop.

② Tochni

MAP E5

Surrounded by vineyards and farmland, Tochni has a traditional feel, with old stone houses lining its narrow streets *(see p42)*.

③ Kalavasos

MAP E5

This village nestles beside a stream in a huddle of old stone houses. Nearby, in the Neolithic village of Tenta, Stone Age skeletons have been found *(see p42)*.

④ Makronissos Tombs

MAP J4 ■ **Open daily**

Cut into the limestone rock are 19 chamber tombs and a religious sanctuary, originally from the Hellenistic era but used by the Romans and Byzantines.

⑤ Deryneia

MAP J4

This farming village looks over to the Turkish-occupied north, towards Famagusta, and you can make out the battlements of the walled city in the distance. An automobile crossing from here to Famagusta is set to open in the near future.

⑥ Sotira

MAP J4

Sotira has five Byzantine churches, the most important of which is Metamorphosis tou Sotiros, from which the village takes its name.

⑦ Liopetri

MAP J4

Woven baskets hanging outside shops here shows that the craft for which this village is famous still thrives.

⑧ Agios Antonios

MAP G4

This ancient hilltop church in Kellia village has some of the oldest (10th–12th century) Byzantine frescoes in Cyprus.

⑨ Hala Sultan Tekke

MAP G5 ■ **Dromolaxia** ■ **Open Apr–Sep: 8:30am–7:30pm daily; Oct–Mar: 8:30am–5pm** ■ **Dis. access**

Hala Sultan Tekke is prettiest in winter and spring when its domes and minaret are reflected in Larnaka's Salt Lake. Within the mosque is the tomb of Umm Haram, aunt of Mohammed.

⑩ Potamos Liopetriou

MAP J4

The tiny port of Liopetri has fishing boats moored along its banks and offers popular fish restaurants.

Boats moored at Potamos Liopetriou

Beaches

Pure white sands at Konnos Bay

1 Konnos Bay
MAP J4

Vegetation covers the steep slopes behind this minute cove, hemmed in by craggy headlands. It is easiest to get to the bay by boat, and it's a popular stop on day-trips from Protaras and Ayia Napa.

2 Mackenzie Beach, Larnaka
MAP G5

Mackenzie (also spelled Makenzy) Beach reportedly owes its name to a Scots caterer who set up a restaurant and bar here just after World War II. It is urban Larnaka's handy beach getaway, much favoured by local families for its grey but clean sand and shallow waters. Lifeguards keep an eye on things, and bar-restaurants line the esplanade behind.

3 Finikoudes, Larnaka
MAP M5

Handy for the sights of central Larnaka, Finikoudes, with its palm-lined pedestrian esplanade, is the ideal place for a cooling swim after a morning's shopping and sightseeing. Very clean for a city beach, it has Blue Flag status and a rank of sun-loungers and umbrellas.

4 Agia Thekla, Ayia Napa
MAP J4

This tiny cove west of Ayia Napa avoids the worst of the summer crowds. There's a small sandy beach guarded by a little white chapel.

5 Makronissos, Ayia Napa
MAP J4

Makronissos's sandy hinterland is perfect for cross-country quad-biking. You can rent bikes at the beach (see p17).

6 Nissi Beach, Ayia Napa
MAP J4

Sleep off the effects of a night's clubbing in the sun at Ayia Napa's most favoured beach or, if you still have the energy, go waterskiing, windsurfing, parascending, jetskiing or even bungee jumping.

7 Kryo Nero, Ayia Napa
MAP J4

Kryo Nero, past Ayia Napa's eastern outskirts, marks the end of the long sandy stretch that begins at Limanaki. A little further along the coast are the spectacular sea caves known as the Thalassines Spilies, where waves have carved grottoes and arches out of the limestone cliffs.

Grottoes near Kryo Nero

8 Fig Tree Bay, Protaras
MAP J4

This crescent of sand, lapped by turquoise waves, is delightful. There is a full menu of water sports.

9 Protaras
MAP J4

The beaches on this part of the coast offer white sand and crystal waters.

10 Louma, Pernera
MAP J4

Only those in the know make it to this sandy stretch of coast – it's the perfect place to escape the crowds.

See map on pp76–7

Bars and Pubs

The Bedrock Inn, Ayia Napa

1 The Bedrock Inn, Ayia Napa

MAP J4 ▪ Ippokratous 2

A colossal Fred Flintstone effigy towers over this loud caveman-themed bar that offers a "silent disco" (using headphones) after 1:30am. Not for the faint-hearted or style conscious.

2 Bikini Beach Bar, Protaras

MAP J4 ▪ Amfitritis 9

You will hear all the latest Greek and international hits here, a popular haunt with local twenty-somethings and visitors alike. It also hosts live events some nights.

3 Guru, Ayia Napa

MAP J4 ▪ Odysseos Elytis 11

Guru is more stylish than the run of Ayia Napa's pubs and bars – it even has a smart-casual dress code. There are three bars, offering a range of bar snacks, and the soundtrack is "fusion ethnic house".

4 Barcode, Ayia Napa

MAP J4 ▪ Georgiou Seferi 17

Located on the main square, this bar is a favourite among locals and tourists alike and a great way to start the evening. The atmosphere is hip and lively and a good range of cocktails are served.

5 Savino Rock Bar, Larnaka

MAP M5 ▪ Watkins 9

A popular lounge bar famous for its black-and-white photos of movie and rock stars that cover the walls. The live rock music is a major draw here.

6 Nissaki Lounge Bar, Ayia Napa

MAP J4 ▪ Nissaki Beach

This bar is popular with locals and has the perfect beachside setting for a sundowner at sunset.

7 Señor Frogs, Ayia Napa

MAP J4 ▪ Agias Mavris 24

Although located slightly out of the town centre, Señor Frogs makes up for it with its lively ambience, impressive playlist, strong drinks list and weekly booze cruise.

8 Pirates Inn, Ayia Napa

MAP J4 ▪ Agias Mavris 1

A convivial atmosphere and inexpensive drinks make this place a favourite start-the-night venue. It usually closes at the end of October with a riotous halloween party.

9 Golden Arrow, Ayia Napa

MAP J4 ▪ Leoforos Archiepiskopou Makariou Tritou 21

Offering large-screen football, and located near Ayia Napa monastery, this is a fun, friendly place with a great range of ale on tap, plus good food.

10 The Queen's Arms, Larnaka

MAP G5 ▪ Larnaka-Dekelia Rd

A long-standing British favourite with a "buy one, get one free" happy hour from 6:30–9:30pm. Beers are on tap, and there's a big-screen TV for watching sports.

Nightspots

1 Carwash, Ayia Napa
MAP J4 ▪ Agias Mavris 24

Unlike many of its rivals on the Ayia Napa nightlife scene, Carwash is primarily a disco. It also sticks to a policy of playing only dance music from the 1970s to the early 1990s.

2 Black N' White, Ayia Napa
MAP J4 ▪ Louka Louka 8

With a playlist focusing on classic soul, hip hop and R&B, this small club is another local institution since 1985.

3 Club Ice, Ayia Napa
MAP J4 ▪ Louka Louka 14

Famed for its R&B nights throughout the summer, which feature big-name DJs from the UK and elsewhere, this is one of the hottest nightspots in Cyprus. An added attraction are the riotous foam and UV paint parties.

4 River Reggae Club, Ayia Napa
MAP J4 ▪ Off Tefkrou Anthia 3

The last place to close its doors for the night in Ayia Napa, the River Reggae Club is the local after-party venue. Take a pre-dawn swim in the pool before watching the sun rise.

5 The Brewery, Larnaka
MAP M5 ▪ Leoforos Athinon 77

This micro-brewery allows you to pull your own pint with pumps at some tables. There is a superb

selection of brews on offer, including lagers and fruity beers, as well as a menu of burgers and fries.

6 Secrets Freedom, Larnaka
MAP G5 ▪ Artemidos 67

The island's biggest gay club (not exclusively so), Secrets Freedom hosts theme parties and occasional drag shows.

7 The Castle Club, Ayia Napa
MAP J4 ▪ Grigoriou Afxentiou

This huge club with several indoor levels and a large outside dance floor offers music by top international DJs.

The Castle Club, Ayia Napa

8 Club Deep, Larnaka
MAP M4 ▪ Leoforos Athinon 30–32

This lively nightclub plays a mix of music from trance to soul and house. There is a massive dance floor and the place gets packed out with a young, energetic crowd.

9 Geometry Club, Larnaka
MAP M5 ▪ Karaoli Dimitriou 8

This stylish venue is a local favourite and the club of choice for 20- to 30-something holidaymakers.

10 Ammos, Larnaka
MAP G5 ▪ Mackenzie Beach

This hip, chilled-out venue combines a restaurant with a rooftop dancefloor and bar. Live events in summer.

The Brewery, Larnaka

See map on pp76–7

Cafés and Eateries

1 Liquid Café, Ayia Napa
MAP J4 ■ Kryou Nerou 19

Chic and spacious, this popular café serves great cocktails as well as gourmet snacks and steaks. Large TV screens show all the sports events of the day.

2 Flames, Ayia Napa
MAP J4 ■ Agias Mavris 58

This long-established family-run eatery serves good, simple fare such as charcoal-grilled chicken, steak and fish. There are plenty of options for vegetarians too.

Souvlaki

3 Stou Fesha, Larnaka
MAP L5 ■ Plateia Agiou Lazarou 20

Visit this first-rate local eatery for lamb chops and other grills. In autumn or winter, you may have to settle for *sheftalia* instead. At night the view from the outdoor tables to Agios Lazaros is unbeatable.

4 Art Café 1900, Larnaka
MAP M5 ■ Stasinou 6

An atmospheric, rambling place with a *belle époque* theme and an intimate atmosphere. The menu is limited, but offers reliable traditional dishes with plenty of vegetarian options and some terrific home-made desserts.

5 Captain Andreas, Ayia Napa
MAP J4 ■ Evagorou 35

This popular taverna in the heart of Ayia Napa, specializes in fresh fish. Owner Captain Andreas can often be seen coming ashore with his catch of the day.

6 Glykolemono, Larnaka
MAP M5 ■ Zinonos Kitieos 105

A classy café in the town centre with antique floor tiling. Enjoy the perfect breakfast with sweet or salty *bougatsa* (custard pie) washed down with meticulously brewed coffee.

7 Pizzeria Pompei, Ayia Napa
MAP J4 ■ Nissi 31

Generally considered the best pizzeria in town, Pizzeria Pompei offers 53 varieties made fresh to order. Great range of cocktails, too.

8 Falafel Abu Dany, Larnaka
MAP M5 ■ Grigoriou Afxentiou 2

Larnaka's large, post-1975 Lebanese community is the source of this much-loved eatery that serves falafel, tabbouleh, hummus, turnovers, soups and other vegetarian dishes.

9 Marios Tavern, Dromolaxia
MAP G5 ■ Eleftherias 18

Excellent *souvlaki* cooked on a charcoal grill with lots of herbs and served in a salad-filled pitta bread. Dishes such as *sheftalia* are also available.

10 Due Pizza, Larnaka
MAP L4 ■ Grigori Afxentiou 11b

Primarily a home-delivery pizzeria, Due Pizza opens in the evening only till 11:30pm.

The quirky interior of Art Café 1900

Restaurants

1 Ploumin, Sotira
MAP J4 ▪ Sotira ▪ 99 658 333 ▪ €

Come here to taste the best *meze* in southeastern Cyprus. The menu changes seasonally, so some goodies such as fennel mushrooms or *kolokasi* (taro root) may not always be on offer. Lovely atmosphere inside a farmhouse with live music three nights every week.

The terrace at Tochni Taverna

2 Tochni Taverna, Tochni
MAP E5 ▪ 24 332 732 ▪ €

The terrace here has pretty views over the valley, and there's a small pool if you want a pre-meal dip.

3 Palazzo Bianco, Ayia Napa
MAP J4 ▪ Aris Velouchiotis 8 ▪ 23 721 942 ▪ €

Specialists in pizza and other Italian dishes, it also serves Mexican fare and grills.

4 Sage, Ayia Napa
MAP J4 ▪ Leoforos Kryou Nerou 8 ▪ 23 819 276 ▪ Dis. access ▪ €€

An elegant restaurant specializing in steaks with a wide choice of sauces. Reservation is recommended.

5 Limelight Taverna, Ayia Napa
MAP J4 ▪ Dimitri Liperti ▪ 23 721 650 ▪ €

Booking is essential at Ayia Napa's most traditional taverna. The best dishes come sizzling from the charcoal grill, including suckling pig, duck, lamb cutlets and lobster.

6 Stou Rousha, Larnaka
MAP M6 ▪ Nikolaou Laniti 26 ▪ 99 243 870 ▪ €

One of the first and best *mageireias* in old Larnaka. Enjoy bean soup, Cypriot ravioli, grills and casserole dishes. Servings are generous but half-portions are available.

7 Monte Carlo, Larnaka
MAP M6 ▪ Piyale Pasha 28 ▪ 24 653 815 ▪ Dis. access ▪ €€

An excellent choice for seafood lovers, head here for delicious fish caught in local waters, served overlooking the sea.

8 Militzis, Larnaka
MAP L6 ▪ Piyale Pasha 42 ▪ 24 655 867 ▪ Dis. access ▪ €

The house speciality here is *kleftiko*, and the characteristic domed ovens that it is prepared in form a part of the decor. You can also opt for *kondosouvli* (slow-roasted pork on a spit) or other grills on offer.

9 Voreas, Voroklini
MAP G4 ▪ Andrea Dimitriou 3 ▪ 24 647 177 ▪ €€

This evening-only taverna excels at grills and *meze*. The dining room has a lovely old-house decor, which looks prettier in winter.

10 Demetrion, Potamos Liopetriou
MAP J4 ▪ 23 991 010 ▪ €€

The smell of fish and hand-cut chips frying in oil greets you as you step in to this breezy, seaside restaurant. Go for by-weight offerings.

See map on pp76–7

🔟 Southwest Cyprus

Home to one of the most cosmopolitan cities, the most upmarket resort town, a UNESCO World Heritage Site that reveals traces of a vanished world, vineyards around mountain villages, plus beaches and wild coasts, southwest Cyprus is the island's most varied region. Limassol and Pafos are lively resorts, with nightlife and activities to match all tastes and a reputation for some of the Mediterranean's best resort hotels, while, wherever you look, there are visible remnants of history, from the Hellenistic mosaics of Kato Pafos to the grand amphitheatre of Kourion and the medieval fortress at Kolossi.

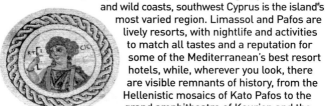

Kato Pafos mosaic

AREA MAP OF SOUTHWEST CYPRUS

Ancient Amathous

1 Ancient Amathous

Standing aloof above the coastal highway east of Limassol, the ruined foundations of Amathous can only hint at its bygone glories. This was one of the very first of the island's city-states – under the Romans it was a provincial capital, while under the Byzantine Empire it was the seat of one of the island's bishops. The remnants of an early Christian basilica, a pagan temple and a spacious Hellenistic agora (marketplace) are the highlights of a site that, despite being close to the luxury resorts and beaches of Limassol's tourist area, is almost always crowd-free (see pp20–21).

- **1** Top 10 Sights
  see pp89–93
- **1** Restaurants
  see p99
- **1** The Best of the Rest
  see p94
- **1** Beaches
  see p95
- **1** Places to Shop
  see p96
- **1** Bars, Pubs and Cafés
  see p98
- **1** Nightspots
  see p97

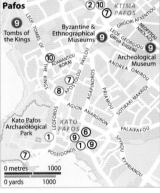

Pafos

Limassol

Battlements of Kolossi Castle

② Kolossi Castle

MAP D6 ■ 14 km (9 miles) west of Limassol ■ Open 8am–5pm daily (to 6pm Apr, May, Sep & Oct; to 7:30pm Jun–Aug) ■ Adm

Kolossi is no fairy-tale fantasy castle, but a solid, forbidding fortress that is testament to the military skills of its medieval builders. For a while, it was a stronghold of the crusading Knights of the Order of St John, and was surrounded by the vineyards from whose grapes they made the celebrated sweet dark amber wine, Commandaria, which was named after their "commandarie". Ransacked by Genoese marauders in the 15th century, it retains many of its original features from that period, thanks to a careful restoration in the 1930s. Highlights of the castle include a private apartment and the coat of arms of one of the commanders. There are great views of the coast from the castle turrets.

③ Historic Limassol

Behind Limassol's waterfront, where palms nod in the breeze in front of modern high-rise buildings, lies a historic city of old-fashioned workshops and markets. Around the bulk of Limassol Castle, built by the island's medieval Lusignan dynasty, are the slender minarets of mosques built in the city's Ottoman heyday, Byzantine churches, narrow shopping streets and a plethora of cafés, bars and restaurants to suit every taste.

The medieval museum, within the castle close to the old harbour, is a must-see, with its gravestones, tableware and Byzantine silver hoard, and there are great rooftop views from the castle battlements. The Central Market, in a graceful arcaded building dating from the British era in the early 20th century, is a great place to shop for items such as handmade reed baskets, virgin olive oil, *loukoumi* (Turkish delight) and other Cypriot delicacies. The market is surrounded by old-fashioned tavernas that make a change from the modern eating-places in the city's resort area (*see pp24–5*).

A café in historic Limassol

④ Carob Mill Museum, Limassol

MAP D6 ■ Vasilissis 1 (by Limassol Castle) ■ 77 777 772 ■ Open daily (times vary – phone to check)

Close to the medieval castle, the Carob Mill Museum is located in a former mill built in 1900. The exhibits clearly show how the carob is harvested, what the fruit is used for and why it has long been an important export for the island. Original machinery used to store and process the fruit and utensils are displayed, along with information panels explaining how they were used. The carob has many uses

See map on pp88–9

CYPRIOT MUSIC

Music and dance are intricately woven into the tapestry of Cypriot life, and traditional instruments, rhythms and melodies are common to both Greek and Turkish Cypriot communities. The key instruments of any village ensemble are the *lyra* or spike fiddle, the five-stringed *bouzouki*, an introduction from Greece, the lute, the violin and the *tampoutsia* frame-drum. All too often, however, tourists are treated to warmed-over versions of film scores such as "Zorba's Dance", played on rather untraditonal electric guitar and synthesizer.

Fasouri Watermania Waterpark

and its pods are a significant source of sugar. The fruit can be found in syrup, sweets and chocolate, while its derivatives are used for making such diverse items as paper, photographic film plates and medicines.

⑤ Sanctuary of Apollo Ylatis

MAP C6 ▪ Limassol–Episkopi road, 3 km (2 miles) west of Kourion ▪ Open Apr–Sep: 8:15am–7:45pm daily; Oct–Mar: 8:15am–5:15pm daily ▪ Adm

Stone fragments and toppled columns mark the site of this 7th century BC shrine to the sun-god Apollo in his role as "Ylatis", or god of the woods and forests. It is one of many examples of the way in which Cyprus blended the deities of each new religion that came to the island with the cults that were already established. The temple has been partially restored by archaeologists and treasures found here are on display in the island's museums.

Sanctuary of Apollo Ylatis

⑥ Fasouri Watermania Waterpark

MAP D6 ▪ Lanitis Fasouri Plantations, Fasouri, Limassol ▪ 25 714 235 ▪ Open May–Oct: 10am–6pm daily ▪ Adm

With its high-speed chutes and slides, interactive games, pools for grown-ups, teens, children and toddlers, Cyprus's largest and most exciting waterpark offers full-on family fun. A very welcome relief from the often blistering heat of high summer, and there are restaurants and shops on site, too *(see p58)*.

Ruins of ancient Kourion, with stunning views of the coast

7 Kourion

Tier after tier of carved stone benches, able to seat up to 3,500 spectators, rise above the circular floor of Kourion's amphitheatre. Nearby, intricate mosaics depict gladiators and mythological characters, as well as fish and birds. These days, the restored theatre is the summer venue for cultural events, including a Shakespeare play in June and concerts later in summer *(see p66)*. Kourion's builders must have had an eye for landscape, too: the theatre has fantastic views over the coast, vineyards and wheat fields of the Akrotiri Peninsula from its position 80 m (260 ft) above sea level *(see pp26–7)*.

8 Akamas Peninsula

The Akamas Peninsula is a bushwhacker's heaven. A four-wheel drive vehicle is needed to reach this rugged spine of hills, covered with pine and juniper trees, but it's worth the effort. Along its western shore are southern Cyprus's most deserted beaches, while from its northern-most tip are fine coastal views. There's excellent snorkelling off its rocky shores, while divers favour the numerous offshore islets, such as St George's Island *(see p49)*. For something less energetic, boat trips are possible from Pafos and Lakki *(see pp32–3)*.

9 Pafos

MAP A5 ■ Tombs of the Kings: Leoforos Tafon ton Vasileon; Open Apr–Sep: 8:30am–7:30pm daily, Oct–Mar: 8:30am–5pm daily; Adm ■ Pafos Ethnographical Museum: Exo Vrysis 1; Open 10am–5pm Mon–Fri, 10am–4pm Sat, 10am–2pm Sun; Adm ■ Pafos Byzantine Museum: Andrea Ioannou 5; Open 9am–3pm Mon–Fri, 9am–1pm Sat; Adm ■ Pafos Archaeological Museum: Leoforos Georgiou Griva Digeni; Open 8am–4pm Mon–Fri; Adm

Pafos is really two towns in one – Kato ("lower") Pafos and Ktima ("upper Pafos"). Kato Pafos was one of the island's most important seaports during the Middle Ages, then fell into decline and languished for centuries until tourism and the rediscovery of its famed mosaics

Coastal views on the Akamas Peninsula

turned it into a burgeoning resort town. Today, luxury hotels are spread along the coast, and a modern centre is packed with souvenir shops, bars, cafés, nightspots and restaurants. Ktima, a mere 3 km (2 miles) inland, seems a world away from the tourist hype, being traditionally Cypriot, with authentic cafés and tavernas that cater to local tastes. There are three museums in Ktima – ethnographical, archaeological and Byzantine – and they are well worth making time to see, each reflecting different eras on the island. West of Ktima, near the sea, lie the eerie, subterranean Tombs of the Kings, hewn out of a rock. Wealthy and aristocratic residents of the ancient city were entombed in these stone chambers from around the 3rd century BC. Despite their name, there is currently no evidence that members of Pafian royalty are buried here.

Tombs of the Kings, Pafos

🔟 Limassol Municipal Folk Art Museum

Housed in a grandiose old merchant's mansion, this museum's collection is almost reminiscent of a jumble sale or an antiques shop. There is an eclectic assemblage of old wooden farm tools and household utensils. There are also silver necklaces and bangles, and decorative, elaborately embroidered and flounced costumes that only a generation ago the local women would have worn on village feast days and special family occasions. It provides a wonderful insight into traditional Cypriot lifestyles *(see p25).*

A MORNING IN PAFOS

▶ Start the day in Ktima or upper Pafos, with a visit to the **Covered Market** *(see p96)*, where you'll find lace, embroidery, ceramics and leather goods and an array of open-air stalls selling everything a traditional Cypriot could wish for, from kebab skewers to fresh fruit and vegetables. From here, walk up to the town's only relic of its Ottoman past, the **Cami Kebir** (Grand Mosque), which began life as the Byzantine church of Agia Sofia.

A stroll back along **Makariou**, Ktima's main street, takes you through the Municipal Gardens with its fountains and cafés to the unassuming **Ethnographical Museum** and, within sight of it, the much more imposing **Byzantine Museum**, housing a large number of post-Byzantine icons. The highlight of its collection is the icon of Agia Marina, dating from the 8th century AD – the oldest known on Cyprus.

In order to avoid a long, hot walk, return to the taxi stand on the town's main square, close to the corner of Makariou and Evagora Pallikaridi streets, and take a five-minute ride to visit the **Archaeological Museum**'s fine collection, which spans the millennia between the Bronze Age and the Byzantine era. Then, having whetted your appetite for ancient arcana, take another cab to **Kato Pafos** *(see pp30–31)* to see the preserved mosaics of this Roman villa complex.

◗ End the morning with a long, cool drink at one of the nearby seafront pavement cafés.

See map on pp88–9

The Best of the Rest

1 Drouseia (Dhrousha)
MAP A4

Overlooked by the limestone crags of Agios Georgios, Drouseia is one of the region's prettiest villages, with old stone houses on steep lanes.

2 Akrotiri Peninsula
MAP D6

The peninsula's salt lake is a refuge in winter for bright pink flamingoes and other migratory birds.

Flamingoes at Akrotiri salt lake

3 Pegeia
MAP A4

Pegeia spreads out from its cobbled central square with a fountain, descending through the fields to the port of Agios Georgios. The latter has a 6th-century Christian basilica featuring a fine mosaic floor with animal and geometric motifs.

4 Pissouri
MAP C6

A hilltop location above a beach lapped by clear blue water makes Pissouri one of the most sought-after addresses on the south coast for expats. A great combination of peace and quiet, choice of places to eat and drink, and low-key nightlife.

5 Chrysorrogiatissa Monastery

MAP B4 ■ Open May–Aug: 9:30am–12:30pm, 1:30–6:30pm daily; Sep–Apr: 10am–12:30pm, 1:30–4pm daily ■ Adm

This monastery produces noteworthy wines. It is also home to a museum of religious items.

6 Palaipafos
MAP B5

This ancient Aphrodite cult sanctuary, by Kouklia village, offers a good museum and a Lusignan manor, which hosts music concerts.

7 Lempa Neolithic Village
MAP A5

Primitive round-houses have been excavated by archaeologists on the site of a Chalkolithic settlement.

8 Palaia Enkleistra
MAP B5

About 4 km (2.5 miles) uphill from Kouklia, this cave-hermitage houses wonderful 15th-century frescoes, including an unusual portrayal of the Holy Trinity. Fetch the key from Palaipafos museum.

9 Polis
MAP A4

Both a farming village and low-key resort, Polis has an uncrowded beach and a small seaport, Lakki, with fish tavernas.

10 Geroskipou
MAP A5 ■ Agia Paraskevi: Open 8am–5pm daily (by warden's permission); Dis. access

Shops selling traditional baskets, ceramics and regional *loukoúmi* (Cyprus Delight) line the main street of this picturesque village on the outskirts of Pafos. On the south side of the main square is the five-domed church of Agia Paraskevi containing mostly 15th-century frescoes.

Agia Paraskevi church, Geroskipou

Beaches

Panorama of pristine Pissouri Bay

1 Pissouri Bay
MAP C6

A bay with clean sand and pebbles, sun-loungers and umbrellas to rent, and a good choice of water sports.

2 Chrysochou Bay, Polis
MAP A4

A beautiful beach with clean pebbles and coarse sand, clear water and great coastal views. In a grove of eucalyptus trees immediately behind the beach there's a camp site with a popular beachside café.

3 Coral Bay
MAP A5

This lovely sandy crescent draws the crowds, especially on summer weekends when it is a magnet for young Cypriots. Turn up early to be sure of finding an empty sun-lounger or a patch of unoccupied sand.

4 Geroskipou
MAP A5

This long beach on the outskirts of Pafos is little used by holidaymakers but is a favourite with locals. It is clean and well tended, with several snack bars behind it, plus showers, sunbeds and changing rooms.

5 Lara Bay
MAP A4

This half-moon stretch to the north of Cape Lara is backed by high dunes and benefits from fine white sand that attracts rare green and loggerhead turtles, who lay their eggs here each summer *(see p33)*.

6 Evdimou
MAP C6

One of the least visited beaches on the south coast. With around 2 km (1.5 miles) of sand and pebbles, it is great for beachcombers looking for solitude. There are two bar-restaurants at either end.

7 Dasoudi
MAP D6

This is the nearest stretch of clean sand and water to central Limassol and justifiably popular with local urbanites as well as holidaymakers.

8 Governor's Beach
MAP E6

White-chalk cliffs are a sharp contrast to the dark sands of this chain of little bays and coves, each with a choice of snack bars and tavernas.

9 Pomos
MAP B3

Low limestone cliffs shelter sandy coves at Pomos, which remains undiscovered by the holiday industry. The water is clean, and with an archipelago of small crags just offshore it's great for snorkelling.

10 Asprokremmos
MAP A4

Some say this is the best beach in Cyprus, and it is certainly one of the least crowded, despite its majestic sweep of sand from which you can gaze out over the sparkling, calm waters or watch splendid sunsets over Cape Amaoutis and its islets.

See map on pp88–9

Places to Shop

1 My Mall, Limassol
MAP D6 ■ Zakaki Junction

This huge shopping mall is located at the northwest entrance to Limassol. Over 150 shops stock everything from high fashion to small gifts. There are also fast-food outlets, a bowling alley and an ice-skating rink.

Central Market, Ktima Pafos

2 Central Market, Ktima Pafos
MAP A5 ■ Agoras

A selection of stalls selling lace, embroidery, handmade leather bags, beachwear and other souvenirs.

3 Pleiades Mosaic Workshop, Laneia
MAP C5

Specializing in colourful mosaics, both copies of famous ancient works and modern originals. They can arrange for larger items to be shipped home.

4 Violet's Second Hand Shop, Limassol
MAP D6 ■ Salaminos 12

This Aladdin's cave of a shop sells a fascinating collection of vintage jewellery, clothing and accessories, including some hand-embroidered Cypriot garments.

5 Cat Kerameas, Limassol
MAP D6 ■ Agkyras 55

This is a good place to shop for unusual, eclectic ceramics by Famagustan potter Andreas Kattos.

6 Fasouri Flea Market
MAP D6 ■ Asomatos ■ Open Sat and Sun

This well-established market has formal stalls selling a variety of items.

7 Cyprus Handicraft Centre, Limassol and Pafos
Limassol: **MAP D6** ■ Themidos 25; Pafos: **MAP A5** ■ Apostolou Pavlou 64

Two government-run stores specialize in island crafts such as laces, baskets and etched gourds.

8 Kings Avenue Mall, Pafos
MAP D6 ■ Leoforos Apostolou Pavlou

This modern shopping centre has around 125 shops and boutiques, as well as cafés, restaurants and a cinema complex.

9 Municipal Market, Limassol
MAP D6 ■ Georgiou Gennadiou

This historic building dates back to 1917 and provides an atmospheric setting for this bustling market where you can find everything from fresh local produce (including honey) to gourmet deli items, Cypriot sweets, flowers and nuts.

10 Panagia's Souvenir Market, Geroskipou
MAP A5 ■ Archiepiskopou Makariou 23

Panagia Athinodorou's shop on the north side of the central square dazzles with its array of brightly painted pottery, bread trays and cane baskets.

Bowls, Panagia's Souvenir Market

Nightspots

A busy bar in Limassol

1 Sto Perama, Limassol
MAP D6 ■ Zik Zak 12–14
This old-town venue near the mosque hosts regular live performances by mainland Greek rock and entechno stars. Good food and bar service make Sto Perama a popular choice.

2 Rialto Theatre, Limassol
MAP D6 ■ Andrea Drousioti 19
Housed in a refurbished 1930s building, this theatre is the south coast's most prestigious venue for musical, dance and theatrical events. It also hosts an annual film festival.

3 The Half Note, Limassol
MAP D6 ■ Sokratous & Saripolou corner
The Half Note hosts live events, including Latin and jazz nights, roughly every month. It attracts a dedicated local crowd who turn up every Friday and Saturday night so arrive early to be sure of getting in.

4 Tepee Strictly Rock Bar, Limassol
MAP D6 ■ Ampelakion 5, Mouttagiaka Junction
This long-established place has an animated, party atmosphere, thanks to the regular line up of live rock bands. A wide range of beers, plus hearty burritos.

5 7-Seas, Limassol
MAP D6 ■ Columbia Plaza, Agiou Andreou 223
This hip venue attracts top international DJs and stages regular live concerts. There are also lively Latino nights and other themed nights held throughout the year.

6 Old Fishing Shack Pub, Kato Pafos
MAP A5 ■ Margarita Gardens, Tefkrou Street
Cyprus's best range of ales and ciders are on offer here. The owner is famed for making his own cider, spiked with ginger, and is happy to make recommendations to novices.

7 Timothy's Art Bar, Ktima Pafos
MAP A5 ■ Off Angelou Geroudi
A bohemian spot tucked away in a Turkish-Cypriot building near the Karavella bus station. It serves Spanish tapas and hosts live world music events (mostly on Fridays).

8 Barrio del Mar, Pafos
MAP A5 ■ Geroskipou Beach
A huge summer venue with indoor and outdoor facilities. There are no fewer than six bars, while the varied music programme ensures the place is always packed.

9 Black and White Reload, Pafos
MAP A5 ■ Agiou Antoniou
Upbeat and cheerful, this Pafos bar pleases visitors with a catchy playlist, affordable drinks and friendly staff.

10 Paradise Place, Pomos
MAP B3 ■ A kilometre west of village centre
You can't miss this building on the inland side of the road. Stop by for a drink or a meal and listen to the eclectic music collection. Hosts regular live events too.

See map on pp88–9

Bars, Pubs and Cafés

1 Flintstones Bar, Pafos
MAP A5 ▪ Dionysou 2

This popular bar attracts a mix of locals and visitors, with music low enough to permit conversation, and a good atmosphere created by the hosts. Offers strong cocktails and free popcorn nibbles.

2 Dino Art Café, Limassol
MAP D6 ▪ Innis 62–66

An ambitious fusion menu (Cypriot, Japanese and international), great coffee and creative desserts are on offer at this quintessential bistro. The contemporary wall art displayed is available to buy.

3 Incontro Café, Limassol
MAP D6 ▪ Archiepiskopou Makariou 244

A stylish venue with bold prints on the walls, crisp white linen on the tables and comfortable sofas to lounge on. This combination of a café, bar, bistro and wine bar also serves light meals.

4 Ibsen Tea & Coffee House, Limassol
MAP D6 ▪ Chrysanthou Mylona 16 ▪ Open 8am–5pm daily

Close to the Archaeological Museum, this place not only serves good tea and coffee, but also wonderful snacks and cakes. Cheerful service.

5 127 Café, Limassol
MAP D6 ▪ Elenis Paleologinas 5

This pleasant café-bar is primarily a hangout spot for the younger generation. It has tables outside in the rear courtyard.

6 The New Horizon, Pafos
MAP A5 ▪ Panareti 3, Coral Bay Rd

Resembling a traditional British pub, this bar has live music events and televised sports, and its standard pub-grub gets rave reviews.

7 La Boite 67, Pafos
MAP A5 ▪ Old Port

As the name suggests, La Boite was founded in 1967 – the first bar in the resort. Once a favourite haunt of art students and local hipsters, it is now a good spot to enjoy a snack or a drink. Prices are affordable considering the location and the staff are welcoming and friendly.

Bustling bar at Draught

8 Draught, Limassol
MAP D6 ▪ Old Carob Mill Complex

The speciality at this bar and grill is cocktails, although a great range of wines and beers (including craft microbrews) is also available.

9 Different Bar, Pafos
MAP A5 ▪ Agiou Antoninou

This is the most gay-friendly bar on the island, but Panos the owner makes all visitors feel welcome. A long-running spot, it stays open throughout winter as well.

10 Tramps Sports Bar, Pafos
MAP A5 ▪ Tafon ton Vasileon 52

Live football and rugby events are screened here. There is also a grill menu and a good range of draught beers.

Restaurants

PRICE CATEGORIES

For a three-course meal for one with half a bottle of wine (or equivalent meal), taxes and extra charges.

€ under €25 €€ €25–€50 €€€ over €50

1 Hondros, Pafos
MAP A5 ■ Leoforos Apostolou Pavlou 96 ■ 26 910 998 ■ €€

One of the oldest restaurants on the island, dating back to 1953, Hondros delivers well-executed Cypriot recipes, plus seafood. Choose from the pleasant outdoor terrace or the cosy eclectically decorated interior.

2 Aliada, Limassol
MAP D6 ■ Eirinis 117 ■ 25 340 758 ■ €€

Set-price buffet is the rule here, and the fare is a mix of Continental and Cypriot. Seating is either in the pretty garden or inside the four rooms of an elegant historic mansion.

3 La Maison Fleurie, Limassol
MAP D6 ■ Christaki Kranou 18 ■ 25 320 680 ■ €€€

This upscale restaurant offers authentic French cuisine, with dishes such as *coq au vin*, *duck à l'orange* (roasted duck served with orange sauce), goose stuffed with *foie gras* and black truffle. Good desserts too.

4 Ariadni's, Vasa
MAP E5 ■ A kilometre south of Vasa village ■ 25 944 064 ■ €

Indulge in Cypriot home-style fare such as *koupepia* with yogurt, black-eyed peas with celery, *anari* cheese turnovers and a range of daily changing mains.

5 Ta Perix, Pafos
MAP A5 ■ Kioubilay 20, Mouttalos, Ktima ■ 99 628 701 ■ €

Pafos's best *meze* restaurant, Ta Perix offers delights such as grilled quail, *pastourmas* (air-dried cured beef), snails and chicken livers.

6 Arsinoë, Polis
MAP A4 ■ Griva Digeni 3 ■ 99 512 037 ■ Closed Sun, winter ■ €€

This long-running fish specialist serves both seafood *meze* and à la carte dishes.

7 7 St Georges, Geroskipou
MAP A5 ■ Georgiou M Savva 37 ■ 99 655 824 ■ €€

Cyprus's most unusual *meze* taverna, this place dishes up platters such as *tsamarella* (goat salami), bladder campion with eggs or fennel mushrooms. The menu changes seasonally.

8 Neon Phaliron, Limassol
MAP D6 ■ Gladstonos 135 ■ 25 365 768 ■ €€

This place is famed locally for giving traditional recipes an up-to-date twist. Game features heavily in winter.

Prawn cocktail at Neon Phaliron

9 Imogen's Inn, Kathikas
MAP A4 ■ 26 633 269 ■ Closed Wed, Nov–Feb ■ €

Imogen's menu reflects Greek and Egyptian cooking in dishes such as *foul madamas* (fava beans stew) or *moutzendra* (lentil/onion risotto).

10 Laona, Pafos
MAP A5 ■ Votsi 6, Ktima ■ 26 937 121 ■ €

Visit this *mageireio* for a traditional lunch consisting of pulse-based dishes, pork with *kolokasi* (taro) and sweets such as *palouzes* (grape-must jelly).

See map on pp88–9

🔟 The Troödos Mountains

Mosaic at the Trooditissa Monastery

Cool breezes waft over the forested slopes of the High Troödos region, making it a perfect refuge from the searing summer heat of Nicosia. Here, the crowded coastal areas seem another world away. The Troödos peaks dominate the horizons of southern Cyprus and, in winter and early spring, when they are often capped with snow, they are at their most spectacular. Modern roads have made the old-fashioned villages here more accessible, but getting to some of the region's world-renowned painted churches often requires long drives on winding roads. There are also many tracks only negotiable by four-wheel drives or mountain bikes.

① Omodos
MAP C5

One of the most popular villages on the tourist trail, the main attraction of the scenic Omodos village is the rambling, atmospheric Timios Stavros monastery, which dominates the vast square. This is also a good place for travellers to buy souvenirs, which range from local wines and food products to embroidery.

The village of Omodos

AREA MAP OF THE TROÖDOS MOUNTAINS

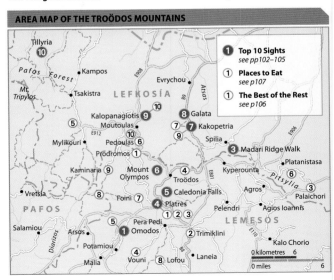

① **Top 10 Sights**
see pp102–105

① **Places to Eat**
see p107

① **The Best of the Rest**
see p106

Previous pages Ruins of St Hilarion Castle, Kyrenia

Interior at Panagia tis Asinou, one of the many painted churches in the region

2 Troödos Painted Churches

Hidden in the high valleys of the remote Troödos, these modest little churches and monastery chapels conceal a treasury of some of the most glorious early Christian works of art in the world. Miraculously, their glowing frescoes have survived the rise and fall of the Byzantine, Ottoman and British empires. Some of them are more than 1,000 years old and in their own way they inspire as much awe as any great cathedral (see pp28–9).

3 Madari Ridge Walk
MAP D4

This wonderful loop-walk can be started from two access points, the more preferable of which is through the minor road between Kyperounta and Spilia villages, where the trail-head is signposted at a pass. The other route starts near the fire lookout on Adelfi peak. Allow three hours to complete the circuit, with time enough to enjoy views over the island, and the dense forest en route. The walk is doable in late winter or early spring, although trails around Mount Olympos may still be blocked by snow.

4 Platres
MAP C5

Situated above a mountain stream that becomes a fierce torrent in winter and spring, Platres is the southern gateway to the Troödos and the most popular spot in the region, with restaurants, souvenir shops and places to stay. It is also a good base for exploring the region, with walking trails and biking tracks branching off in all directions, and a cool climate even in high summer. The village is made up of two districts: Pano (Upper) Platres, the main resort, and traditional Kato (Lower) Platres.

Mountain stream near Platres

ICONS AND FRESCOES

The names of almost all the artists who painted the icons and frescoes of the Troödos churches are unknown. Legends claim many of the oldest icons "flew" to Cyprus of their own accord in the 8th century to escape destruction by a purist Christian sect, the Iconoclasts ("icon breakers"). Common themes for the frescoes include the Crucifixion and Resurrection, and the Last Judgement, with halo-wearing saints and martyrs, grinning demons, crimson dragons and Roman soldiers.

Fresco in the Archangelos Michael church

 Caledonia Falls
MAP C5

Tumbling into a wooded ravine, this 11-m (36-ft) waterfall is at its most spectacular in spring, when the Troödos streams are fed by melting snow. It is most popular in summer, when it offers a cool, shady retreat from the powerful midday sun. Its name derives from the swallows (chelidonia) which chase insects above its pool on summer evenings (see p54).

The snowy peak at Mount Olympos

 Mount Olympos
MAP C4

Visit the highest peak of the Troödos range for fantastic views over the mountains and down to the sea. It provides a welcome breath of cool mountain air in summer and, from January to early March, it's a skier's delight. The 1,952-m (6,404-ft) peak shares its name with the much higher mountain that was the legendary home of Zeus and the rest of the ancient gods on mainland Greece,

and with other summits in the Greek islands and Asia Minor. It is also known as Chionistra or "the snowy one" (see p54).

 Kakopetria
MAP D4

The name of this village translates as "wicked rock-pile" and it's not difficult to see why, when one looks out over the harsh surrounding landscape. Despite the ominous introduction, Kakopetria is actually a pretty and prosperous village and a favourite getaway spot for Nicosian weekenders (see p43). It also makes a good base for exploring many of the remarkable Troödos painted churches that can be found nearby.

 Galata
MAP D4

The precarious-looking balconies of handsome village houses overhang the main street of this old-fashioned

Picturesque Galata village

community that is about 2 km (1 mile) downstream from Kakopetria, which is located beside the same mountain stream. Galata has four painted churches: Panagia tis Podithou *(see p29)*, Archangelos, Agios Sozomenos and Panagia Theotokou.

9 Agios Ioannis Lampadistis

MAP C4 ■ Open 8am–1pm & 2–4pm Tue–Sat, 10am–1pm & 2–4pm Sun (to 7pm in summer)

Unique among the island's monasteries, Agios Ioannis Lampadistis was built near a sacred sulphurous spring. Ever since its 11th-century foundation, the monastery has changed little, retaining its cells and outbuildings. Frescoes from the 13th to 15th centuries cover the walls of the three separate chapels under one roof here.

Mouflon on a mountainside

10 Tillyria
MAP C3

Cyprus's last real stretch of mountain and forest wilderness is a vast tract of pine-covered hillsides that slope down from the western flank of the Troödos range towards the beaches of the northwest coast. The region is criss-crossed with numerous nature trails and is one of the very few areas where attentive walkers might be lucky enough to catch a fleeting glimpse of one of the seven hundred mouflon (horned wild sheep) still surviving in their natural habitat. There are only two paved roads from Kykkos Monastery that cross Tillyria: one goes to Pachyammos and the other towards Kato Pyrgos. Also note that there is usually no mobile network.

A MORNING HIKE ON MOUNT OLYMPOS

Although the summit of **Mount Olympos** can be reached by car, hiking to the peak on foot offers a greater sense of achievement. Start from the **Troödos** resort car park and follow the sign-posted **Atalante Trail**, which is waymarked by strategically positioned red dots. Following the 1,750-m (5,740-ft) contour, this is an undemanding walk for most of the way, through pine and juniper woods, where birds and butterflies flit, and with glimpses of the sea and the plains far below. Covering a little over 16 km (10 miles) and only about 200 m (656 ft) in altitude, this walk can be completed in a morning by anyone of reasonable fitness, but comfortable trainers or walking boots, plus water and – especially in summer – a hat and sunblock are musts.

After around three hours, the so-called Atalante Trail connects with the **Artemis Trail** *(see p53)*. Detour upwards to the summit (you can't miss the giant radar globes and telecom towers) then loop back down to Troödos resort. En route you will pass mineral formations and information markers set up by the tourist office that point out the indigenous wildlife and plants of the region. In spring, look out for crocuses and anemones.

At the summit are the ruins of a 16th-century Venetian fortress, built in a futile attempt to defend the island against the invading Ottomans *(see p36)*.

Your walk completed, enjoy a lunch of fresh trout at a restaurant in **Pano Platres**.

See map on p102

The Best of the Rest

1 Prodromos
MAP C4

The highest settlement in Cyprus, at 1,440 m (4,725 ft) above sea level, the quaint village of Prodromos commands the pass between Mount Olympus in the east and Agios Ilias in the west. It stands among cherry and apple orchards smothered in blossom in spring and early summer.

2 Trimiklini
MAP D5

The church of Panagia Trikoukiotissa is all that remains of this monastery built in the 13th century. The church contains an icon of the Virgin which is credited with the ability to bring rain to parched fields.

3 Palaichori
MAP E4

This large, easterly Troödos village preserves two frescoed, 16th-century churches: the UNESCO-listed Metamorfosi tou Sotiriou *(see p28)* and Chrysopantanassa.

4 Almyrolivado
MAP D4

The focal point of this hillside spot is a giant juniper tree, said to be the oldest tree on the island.

5 Tomb of Makarios
MAP C4

Sentries keep watch around the clock outside the mountain-top tomb of

Tomb of Makarios

Archbishop Makarios III *(see p37)*. From the summit you can see for miles across the Tillyrian forests.

6 Pitsylia Region
MAP D4

Vines, almonds and hazelnuts are the mainstay crops of these pretty hill-farming villages.

Hillside crops in the Pitsylia region

7 Foini
MAP C5 ■ Museum: Open 10am–1pm daily; Adm

Foini is famous for its lovely ceramics and its Pilavakio Museum displays pottery and other rural paraphernalia.

8 Elia Venetian Bridge
MAP C5

This arched stone river bridge – the highest in the Troödos – is testament to the skills of the Venetians, who opened a caravan route through these hills.

9 Kaminaria
MAP C4

Kamanaria is home to the 16th-century chapel of Panagia, which preserves Lusignan-influenced frescoes.

10 Marathasa Valley
MAP C4

The hill villages of Pedoulas and Moutoulas are gateways to the dramatic Marathasa Valley, covered with cherry orchards.

Places to Eat

PRICE CATEGORIES

For a three-course meal for one with half a bottle of wine (or equivalent meal), taxes and extra charges.

€ under €25 **€€** €25–€50 **€€€** over €50

① Village Tavern, Platres
MAP C5 ▪ Makariou 26 ▪ 25 422 777 ▪ €

This traditional taverna is an ideal year-round choice: in warm weather there are tables outside under a shady terrace, and in the cooler months there is a large, cosy indoor dining room. The menu features a *meze*-type medley of starters, plus main courses of the day.

② Psilo Dendro Trout Farm Restaurant
MAP C5 ▪ Psilo Dendro Canyon ▪ 25 813 131 ▪ €

Trouts are netted out fresh from the fish tanks upon ordering and served at your table. The place gets packed out during summer, so book ahead.

③ To Anoi, Platres
MAP C5 ▪ 25 422 900 ▪ €

A typically Cypriot hybrid of English-style pub and traditional café, with cold beer and soft drinks, kebabs and other light meals, and a range of sandwiches and ice creams on offer.

④ Takis Taverna, Vouni
MAP C5 ▪ Vouni Village centre ▪ 25 943 631 ▪ €

There is no written menu at this taverna; just a daily-changing, *meze*-medley for a set price. Book ahead, especially on Sunday afternoon when there is live acoustic music.

⑤ Katoi, Omodos
MAP C5 ▪ 99 674 444 ▪ €€

Opt for the *meze*, accompanied by a glass of local wine at this popular restaurant. There are two arcaded indoor halls and two outdoor dining spaces, but you still need to reserve in advance, especially on weekends.

⑥ Platanos, Pedoulas
MAP C4 ▪ 22 952 518 ▪ €

An old-fashioned *exohiko kendro* (rural taverna) under a plane tree in a quiet corner of Pedoulas. Serves traditional Cypriot cuisine.

⑦ Tziellari, Kakopetria
MAP D4 ▪ 22 922 522 ▪ Closed Mon–Wed winter ▪ €€

This small but cosy restaurant is set inside a converted village house. The food reflects the owner's Argentine background, with massive grills and empanadas on offer.

⑧ Lofou Taverna, Lofou
MAP C5 ▪ 25 470 202 ▪ €

Enjoy generous if not innovative *meze* at this old-style, arcaded taverna. If you are lucky, the owner Kostas and his friends might play guitars or mandolins to entertain you. The place, however, gets busy on weekends.

Lofou Yaverna, Lofou

⑨ Mylos Restaurant, Kakopetria
MAP D4 ▪ Mill Hotel ▪ 22 922 536 ▪ Closed Nov & Dec ▪ Dis. access ▪ €€

This place serves Cypriot starters and international dishes, but the star of the show is their signature trout.

⑩ To Palio Sinema, Kalopanagiotis
MAP D4 ▪ Markou Drakou 40 ▪ 99 130 275 ▪ €

"The Old Cinema" is now a welcoming restaurant offering Cypriot fare in generous portions.

See map on p102

🔟 Northern Cyprus

Palm trees, minarets, mosques and the ruins of Crusader castles and medieval churches built in the Lusignan-Venetian heyday all contribute to Northern Cyprus's old-world ambience. Quite separate from the Republic of Cyprus, as a result of the international boycott imposed on the north since 1974, life here proceeds at a gentler pace than in the south. Here there are empty beaches to bask on, colonial tracks in rugged mountains with views out to sea, and small harbours where old-fashioned fishing boats line quays crammed with the tables of lively fish restaurants.

Detail of a window from the Selimiye Mosque

Fishing boats moored at Kyrenia harbour

AREA MAP OF NORTHERN CYPRUS

1 North Nicosia
MAP P2

Crumbling old houses and a cheerful clutter of bazaars surround the medieval monuments of the Turkish-Cypriot half of the divided city. The Selimiye Mosque – a picturesque hybrid of medieval Christian and Islamic architecture – is the city's most prominent landmark.

2 Kyrenia
MAP F2

Beneath the jagged watershed of the Kyrenia range, this city is set around and above a superb natural harbour. It is dominated by the battlements of a massive Venetian sea fort that withstood assault for centuries until, in 1570, its defenders surrendered to the Ottomans. Northern Cyprus's best hotels are found nearby *(see pp130–31)*.

3 St Hilarion Castle
MAP E2 ■ Open Jun–Oct: 9am–4:45pm daily; Nov–May: 9am–1pm, 2–4:45pm ■ Adm

Constructed by the Lusignans atop a Byzantine fort, St Hilarion has elaborate defences built around mountain

Bellapais Abbey cloister

crags. There are legends of a hidden treasure room and an enchanted garden, and tales of Byzantine treachery and medieval intrigue. It was last occupied in the 20th century by Turkish-Cypriot fighters.

4 Bellapais Abbey
MAP F2 ■ Open Jun–Oct: 9am–6:45pm daily; Nov–May: 9am–1pm, 2–4:45pm ■ Adm

Bellapais justifies the journey just for its sea views. But the abbey, founded by the Augustinian order around 1200, also has Cyprus's most spectacular Gothic architecture in Cyprus. Highlights are the 14th-century cloister and a magnificent refectory.

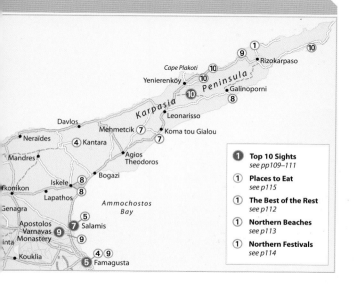

1	**Top 10 Sights** see pp109–111
1	**Places to Eat** see p115
1	**The Best of the Rest** see p112
1	**Northern Beaches** see p113
1	**Northern Festivals** see p114

Former cathedral, Famagusta

5 Medieval Famagusta
MAP J4

Within Venetian ramparts, Famagusta (Gazimağusa) conceals Gothic and Islamic architectural gems. At its heart is the Lala Mustafa Paşa Mosque, originally St Nicholas Cathedral, with its Gothic porticoes and rose window. Huge stone cannonballs, relics of the ten-month siege of the city in 1570–71, lie in the streets. Overlooking the harbour is the "Othello Tower", so called because Famagusta was supposedly the setting for Shakespeare's play.

6 Kyrenia Castle
MAP F2 ■ Open Jun–Oct: 9am–7pm daily; Nov–May: 9am–1pm, 2–4:45pm daily ■ Adm

Within Kyrenia Castle is the Shipwreck Museum, housing the world's oldest wrecked ship – sunk around 300 BC and salvaged in 1967 – complete with its ancient cargo. Also here is the fascinating Tomb-Finds Gallery, which displays Neolithic, Bronze Age and Hellenistic treasures.

HISTORY OF SALAMIS

Salamis was first settled by Mycenaean Greeks, and by the 5th century BC it had become the most important city-state on the island. Its kings resisted the Persian empire and became allies of Alexander the Great, but after his death the city was conquered by Ptolemy I. After Christianity came to Cyprus it became once again the island's capital. A series of natural disasters in the 4th century led to its decline, and the city vanished beneath the sand. It was rediscovered by archaeologists (**right**) but excavations were interrupted by the events of 1974, and more of the site remains to be unearthed.

7 Salamis
MAP J3 ■ Open Jun–Oct: 9am–7pm daily; Nov–May: 9am–1pm, 2–4:45pm daily ■ Adm

Graceful columns, rising from a honeycomb of toppled walls, mark the site of the greatest of Cyprus's ancient cities. Founded more than 3,000 years ago, Salamis dominated the island until its near-destruction by earthquakes in the 4th century AD. Archaeologists have found Hellenistic mosaics, the remains of Roman baths, a handsome amphitheatre and the foundations of two large Byzantine basilicas.

Kyrenia Castle

8 Buffavento Castle

MAP F3 ■ Open daily (hours may vary due to military occupation)

Almost 1,000 m (3,280 ft) above sea level, Buffavento's dilapidated square tower and keep were built by the Byzantines to watch for Saracen raiders and alert the defenders of Kyrenia. Long abandoned, its windy battlements offer breathtaking views of the coast, especially at dusk with the lights of Nicosia lighting up the horizon.

9 Apostolos Varnavas Monastery

MAP H3 ■ Open Jun–Oct: 9am–7pm daily; Nov–May: 9am–1pm, 2–4:45pm ■ Adm

This imposing monastery with its sturdy dome was built in 1756, but its main attraction for Orthodox pilgrims is a much older relic: the catacomb-tomb of Barnabas, a Salamis native who evangelised Cyprus. Since 1974, the monastery's cells have become Northern Cyprus's main archaeological museum, in which Bronze Age pottery items are the star exhibits.

Apostolos Varnavas Monastery

10 Karpasia Peninsula

MAP K2

This long, rugged spit of land, also known as Karpaz Peninsula, is the least developed part of the island, with sandy beaches on both the coasts and a scattering of historic Christian churches, including the monastery of Apostolos Andreas, which is being restored with UN funding. Within it is a holy well much esteemed for its healing properties.

A MORNING IN NORTH NICOSIA

Enter **North Nicosia** *(see p109)* via the **Ledra Street** pedestrian crossing and browse through the stalls at this medina-like market before heading to **Atatürk Meydanı**, the hub of the old town. Southeast of here, historic buildings tower above a maze of narrow, winding streets.

Walk down **Asmaaltı Sokağı** to the fortress-like **Büyük Han**, a 16th-century *kervanaray* with an arcaded courtyard, which now houses artists' studios, handicraft shops and a pleasant café, then turn left towards the soaring Gothic front of the **Selimiye Camii**. This 700-year-old cathedral of **Agia Sofia** (Holy Wisdom) turned mosque is North Nicosia's greatest glory. Behind it, signs lead you to a small square, **Selimiye Meydanı**, and the Sultan Mahmut Library, an eight-sided building with a domed roof containing a collection of Islamic manuscripts and ancient Korans. On the opposite side of the square, a collection of stonework in the **Lapidary Museum** includes medieval crests, Turkish tombstones and gargoyles stripped from the Gothic cathedral.

South of the Selimiye is another Gothic relic, the **Church of St Nicholas**, which became a storehouse under the Ottomans. Walk north from the Selimiye to reach the **Haydarpaşa Camii**, which was originally the Lusignan church of St Catherine. It opens occasionally as an exhibit venue.

Take a leisurely stroll back through the Arabahmet quarter, and enjoy lunch at the **Boghjalian Konak Restaurant** *(see p115)*.

See map on pp108–9

The Best of the Rest

1 Agios Filon
MAP L1 ■ Karpasia Peninsula

The most romantic ruin in Northern Cyprus, Agios Filon (Ayfilon) is a historic, 10th-century chapel, flanked by Washingtonia palms and featuring opus sectile flooring.

2 Kyrenia Folk Art Museum
MAP F2 ■ Open Jun–Oct: 9am–2pm daily; Nov–May: 9am–1pm, 2–4:45pm daily ■ Adm

Traditional implements from the area are on display here. Many, such as the wooden olive-oil press and threshing sledge, were in use only a generation ago.

3 Vouni
MAP C3 ■ Open summer: 10am–5pm daily; winter: 9am–1pm & 2–4:45pm daily ■ Adm

This mysterious hilltop palace, built around 480 BC, was a pro-Persian stronghold with a sophisticated drainage system. Its cliff-top location offers stunning views of the Mediterranean.

4 Kantara Castle
MAP J2 ■ Open summer: 10am–4:45pm daily; winter: 9am–1pm & 2–4:45pm daily

This historic castle commands the eastern end of the Kyrenia range. The most intact surviving portions are the southeast tower, barracks and the northeast bastion.

The ruins of Kantara Castle

5 Soloi
MAP C3 ■ Open summer: 9am–7pm daily; winter: 9am–1pm & 2–4:45pm daily ■ Adm

Mosaics of dolphins and birds adorn the basilica of this Bronze Age-town.

6 Lefka
MAP C3

Lefka feels like an oasis with citrus groves and date palms, the latter surrounding Piri Osman Paşa Mosque.

7 Antifonitis Monastery
MAP G2 ■ Open summer: 9am–2pm daily; winter: 9am–1pm, 2–4:45pm daily

A painted *Pantokrator* (Christ) gazes down from the dome of this otherwise vandalised 12th-century church.

8 Iskele (Trikomo)
MAP J3 ■ Panagia Theotokos: Geçitkale Rd ■ Open 9am–5pm daily ■ Adm

This town's Byzantine church features 12th–15th century frescoes.

9 Royal Tombs
MAP J3 ■ Open Jun–Oct: 9am–7pm daily; Nov–May: 9am–1pm, 2–4:45pm daily ■ Adm

These Bronze Age graves contained objects intended to accompany kings into the afterlife. Most are now in the Cyprus Museum *(see pp14–15)*.

10 Agia Trias (Sıpahı)
MAP K1

Incredible 5th-century mosaics adorn a three-naved basillica here.

Northern Beaches

 Salamis
MAP J3

Visitors to Salamis *(see p110)* can combine sightseeing with sunbathing at the long beach next to the ancient site. A reef protects shallow, clear water – good for snorkelling.

 Acapulco Beach
MAP F2

This beautiful beach is Northern Cyprus's most popular stretch of sand and on summer weekends you certainly won't be alone – Turkish Cypriots from Nicosia flock here to escape the scorching heat of the city. Facilities include a dedicated resort complex, water sports and restaurants.

 Beşinci Mil (5th Mile)
MAP E2

This small beach at Karaoglanoglou has fine sand, gentle shelving, sun-beds and a landmark offshore rock that's easy to reach.

Acapulco Beach, a popular spot

 Paloura
MAP K2

A couple of basic snack bars and one hotel complement Paloura's stretch of golden sand and clear blue water.

 Lara
MAP F2

Jagged rocks frame Lara's pristine stretch of sand, which is usually much less busy than Acapulco. It has a couple of bar-restaurants serving snacks and cold drinks.

 Skoutari
MAP L2

A long stretch of sand and pebbles midway along the Karpasia Peninsula's south coast. Not far offshore, there is great snorkelling around tiny Kilas Island.

 Alagadi Halk Plaji
MAP G2

Endangered loggerhead and green turtles lay their eggs on this unspoiled crescent of sand and shingle. The Society for Protection of Turtles (SPOT) shelters and nurtures eggs and hatchlings. It operates a small information centre and takes visitors on turtle-watching walks from May to October, during nesting season. There are several restaurants nearby.

 Ronnas
MAP L1

A large, empty beach on the northern shore of the Karpasia Peninsula, overlooked by pine woods. It is another nesting place for endangered green turtles.

Nankomi, or "Golden Beach"

 Onüçüncü Mil (13th Mile)
MAP G2

One of Northern Cyprus's best options, just past Alagadi, this stretch of coast offers an arc of almost deserted, fine sand, with grassy dunes, pine trees and craggy limestone headlands.

Nankomi
MAP M1

"Golden Beach" lives up to its nickname – 5 km (3 miles) of south-facing golden sand backed by dunes in Karpasia Peninsula.

See map on pp108–9

Northern Festivals

Güzelyurt Orange Festival

1 International Bellapais Music Festival

May–Jun

The refectory of Bellapais Abbey comes alive every year during this season of classical concerts, which attract musicians and music-lovers from all over the world.

2 Güzelyurt Orange Festival

Jun

Since 1977, Güzelyurt (Morphou) in Northern Cyprus's citrus-growing region has been the venue for a festival that originally celebrated the orange harvest. It has now expanded to include concerts, competitions and art exhibitions.

3 Lapta Tourism Festival

Jun

Folk dance performances by international groups and Turkish music concerts are the highlights of this festival, which is held over several days.

4 Gazimağusa Famagusta Art & Culture Festival

Jun–Jul

This well-established event features music concerts by Turkish performers and international artists. It's held at the ancient theatre in Salamis.

5 Theatre Festival

Sep

This top-flight drama festival, held at the Atatürk Congress Hall of the Near East University in North Nicosia, features around eight performances.

6 Kyrenia Olive Festival

Oct

Traditional folk musicians and costumed dancers help celebrate the olive harvest, and plenty of food and drink is laid out in Zeytinlik village. Most events take place at Kyrenia Castle (see p110).

7 Mehmetcik Grape Festival

Jul–Aug

In Karpasia's main vine-growing region, the village of Mehmetcik marks each successful wine-producing season with music and dancing, along with grape sucuk (a Cypriot sweet) and wine or zivania.

8 Iskele (Trikomo) Festival

Jul

Costume balls, a parade, car rallies and a beauty contest are the staples of this festival.

9 Kurban Bayramı

Dates vary according to the Islamic calendar

This event commemorates the thwarted sacrifice of Ishamael by Abraham (an Islamic version of the Abraham-Isaac story) and is marked by the roasting of sheep.

10 Şeker Bayramı (Sugar Festival)

Dates vary according to the Islamic calendar

Feasts and family reunions mark the end of the annual Ramazan fast. Everyone dons new clothes and makes up for a month of abstinence, especially on Arife, the first evening of the festival.

Places to Eat

1 Şeher'de Meyhane, North Nicosia

MAP P2 ▪ Şehit Ecvet Yusuf Caddesi ▪ 533 862 0606 ▪ €€

Among the best *meyhanes* (taverna) of North Nicosia, this eatery serves great food and a range of premium *raki* (Turkish alcoholic drink).

2 Jashan, Kyrenia

MAP F2 ▪ Karaoğlanoğlu Caddesi ▪ 0392 822 20 27 ▪ €€€

Head to this delightful venue to get a taste of Indian, Pakistani and Bangladeshi cuisines.

3 Archway, Kyrenia

MAP F2 ▪ Zeytinlik (Templos) village centre ▪ 0392 816 03 53 ▪ €€

Set amid mock-rustic surroundings, Archway is one of the best dining options for non-vegetarians in the area. Choose between kebabs and à la carte grills. Good wine list.

Outdoor dining at Sedirhan, Nicosia

4 Anı, Çatalköy

MAP F2 ▪ Şehit Zeka Adil Caddesi ▪ 0392 824 43 55 ▪ €€

One of the best fish restaurants near Kyrenia, this place also offers *meze* starters apart from the regular fish dishes. Pre-order their speciality, *lahoz* (white grouper) baked in salt.

5 Old Grapevine Restaurant, Kyrenia

MAP F2 ▪ Ecevit Caddesi ▪ 0392 815 24 96 ▪ €€

An amiable British-influenced spot with a pub-like atmosphere, the Old

PRICE CATEGORIES
For a three-course meal for one with half a bottle of wine (or equivalent meal), taxes and extra charges.

€ under €25   €€ €25–€50   €€€ over €50

Grapevine is one of Kyrenia's social hubs. The interior is atmospheric and the food estimable.

6 Yorgo Kasap, Kormakitis

MAP D2 ▪ Kormakitis (Koruçam) village centre ▪ 0392 724 20 60 ▪ €€

A Maronite-run taverna, Yorgo Kasap offers a *meze*-only menu, focused on superb *kleftiko*. It's a great lunch option en route to Soloi or Vounoi.

7 Boghjalian Konak Restaurant, Nicosia

MAP N2 ▪ Salahi Sevket Sok, Arabahmet ▪ 0392 228 07 00 ▪ €€€

The only restaurant in the Arabahmet district serves lavish *meze* in an old courtyard, a private dining room or an Ottoman-style banquet room upstairs.

8 Sedirhan, Nicosia

MAP P2 ▪ Büyük Han ▪ 0392 228 77 60 ▪ Dis. access ▪ €

Sedirhan's prime attraction is its charming location in the Büyük Han courtyard. Soak in the views while enjoying snacks such as *börek* (baked stuffed pastries) or a glass of beer.

9 Gingko, Famagusta

MAP J4 ▪ Next to Lala Mustafa Paşa Mosque ▪ 0392 366 66 60 ▪ €

The setting alone, inside a former medrese with medieval domes and arches, calls for a visit here. Good international fare.

10 Alevkayalı, Karpasia

MAP K1 ▪ Aytheriso Shrine, near Yenierenköy ▪ 0392 815 87 15 ▪ €

Karpasia is known for the best fish in Cyprus, and Alevkayalı is the most reliable purveyor. Enjoy great sunset views from the terrace while dining.

See map on pp108–9

Streetsmart

Limassol street cafés

Getting To and Around Cyprus

Arriving by Air

Two airports handle international flights to The Republic of Cyprus: **Larnaka Airport** and **Pafos Airport**. Numerous European airlines fly to both airports from many cities across Europe. There are also charter flights available, generally block-booked by package tour companies and including accommodation with half- or full-board and airport transfer. Some fly all year round, but the majority operate only from April to October. Full service airlines tend to fly into Larnaka while budget carriers favour Pafos. Prices depend on the season and are most expensive from July to September.

For travellers from the UK, budget airlines can offer excellent prices. Both **EasyJet** and **Ryanair** offer inexpensive flights to Larnaka and Pafos from several UK airports.

Flights to Cyprus from the USA always include a stop in Europe en route and occasionally a change of airline.

Regular buses run from Larnaka Airport to the city's central bus station, and the journey will take approximately 15 minutes. Pafos is similarly served by local buses which leave roughly half hourly to the harbour in Kato Pafos; a distance of some 8 km (5 miles). There is one airport in Northern Cyprus: **Ercan Airport**, located 14 km (9 miles) east of North Nicosia. However this airport is not recognized by international airline authorities, so it is not possible to fly there direct. Instead, airlines must touch down in Turkey before continuing on to Ercan. The two airlines flying to Ercan are **Turkish Airlines** which connects Northern Cyprus with Istanbul, Ankara and other Turkish cities and **Pegasus Airlines**. Many visitors to Northern Cyprus fly to Larnaka Airport and cross the border as these flights tend to be more reliable and less subject to delays. Such travellers must arrange a van shuttle to Northern Cyprus.

The easiest way to visit Northern Cyprus is on a package holiday which offers a combination of flights, accommodation, airport transport and, generally, car hire. Lists of specialist tour operators offering package holidays are available from the **North Cyprus Tourism Centre** *(see p123)*.

Most charter flights to Northern Cyprus are intended to be sold as part of a holiday package, but some "flight-only" deals are available and are the best bet for those travelling on a budget. As with scheduled flights, all charter flights to Northern Cyprus must first land in Turkey.

Arriving by Sea

The only way to arrive in the Republic of Cyprus by sea is on a cruise liner as no passenger ferries call at Southern Cypriot ports. Cyprus is the cruising gateway to the Eastern Mediterranean and the Middle East, but due to security considerations travel is restricted to Lebanon and Israel only. The main arrival and depar-ture port in the south is Limassol's new port, 4 km (2.5 miles) southwest of the town centre.

Slow (six-hour) car ferries travel between Taşucu on the Turkish Mediterranean coast, and Kyrenia in Northern Cyprus. Choose between slower car ferries or faster sea-buses.

Travelling by Car

Driving is the easiest way to get around Cyprus. Roads are generally good, with motorways connect-ing Nicosia with Larnaka, Limassol, Pafos and Agia Napa. Distances are short – it is less than 160 km (100 miles) from Pafos to Nicosia. Road distances are in kilometres only and signage is in Greek and Latin in the Republic of Cyprus while in Northern Cyprus all signs are in Turkish only.

Car hire companies have offices in all four major towns in the south (Nicosia, Larnaka, Pafos and Limassol) and at Larnaka and Pafos air-ports. Drivers should be aged 21 or over in the Republic of Cyprus, and 18 or over in Northern Cyprus. A full national or international driving licence is required, and drivers under 25 may need additional insurance cover. Note that both the

Republic of Cyprus and Northern Cyprus issue full car insurance when you rent a car, but Northern Cyprus also has a specific third-party insurance for cars driven into Northern Cyprus from the south. Southern car rental companies specifically forbid you from taking their vehicles in the north.

By Bus

In the Republic of Cyprus, each of the districts operates its own bus company. Fares are government subsidised and cheap. There are also intercity buses, with some discounts on return trips. Local buses connect outlying villages with the nearest town, but departures are only in the early morning/mid-afternoon.

Buses in Northern Cyprus are operated by private operators. Check with the **North Cyprus Tourism Centre** (see p123) for further information. Single tickets can be bought on the bus, but for multiple fares, purchase your tickets at the nearest bus station.

By Taxi

Taxis are plentiful throughout the island and can be hailed from the street or at a taxi rank, or booked on the phone. They are generally comfortable and air-conditioned. Meters are not generally used in Northern Cyprus so it is important to establish the fare before you set off. Service taxis are shared taxis which go between towns.

By Bicycle

Cycling is an enjoyable way of exploring the island, but it is important to remember that it is not ideal in mid-summer when heatstroke is a real risk. **The Cyprus Tourism Organisation (CTO)** (see p123) in Southern Cyprus has a *Cyprus for Cycling* brochure that maps out 19 mountain bike rides across the south of the island. In the south, most towns have bicycle lanes, including major resorts such as Agia Napa, Larnaka, Limassol and Pafos. In the north, however, they barely exist and, overall there are fewer cyclists on the road. Bicycle rental is available throughout the island, however.

DIRECTORY

AIRPORTS
Ercan Airport
🅦 flyercan.com

Larnaka Airport
🅦 cyprusairports.com.cy

Pafos Airport
🅦 cyprusairports.com.cy

AIRLINES
Aegean Airlines
🅦 aegeanair.com

British Airways
🅦 britishairways.com

EasyJet
🅦 easyjet.com

Pegasus Airlines
🅦 flypgs.com

Ryanair
🅦 ryanair.com

Turkish Airlines
🅦 turkishairlines.com

BUSES
EMEL
🅦 limassolbuses.com

InterCity Buses
🅦 intercity-buses.com

Osea
🅦 osea.com.cy

Osel
🅦 osel.com.cy

Osypa
🅦 pafosbuses.com

Zinonas
🅦 zinonasbuses.com

FERRIES
Akgünler Denizcilik
🅦 akgunlerbilet.com

Direct Ferries
🅦 directferries.co.uk

TAXIS AND TRANSFERS–SOUTH
Acropolis Taxi
🅦 acropolis-transport. com

CyprusNet
🅦 cyprustaxi.com

George Cyprus Taxi
🅦 georgecyprustaxi.com

Travel & Express (Service Taxi)
🅦 travelexpress.com.cy

TAXIS AND TRANSFERS–NORTH
Kyrenia Taxi
🅦 Kyreniataxiservice.com

Young Taxi
🅦 youngtaxi.com

CAR HIRE
Budget
🅦 budget.com.cy

Elephant
🅦 elephantrentacar.com

Hertz
🅦 hertz.com.cy

Sun Rent a Car
🅦 sunrentacar.com

BICYCLE HIRE
Cycle in Cyprus
🅦 cycle-in-cyprus.com

MTB Cyprus
🅦 mountainbikecyprus. com

Practical Information

Passports and Visas

Most visitors, including citizens of the EU, the USA, Canada, Australia and New Zealand, do not need a visa to visit the Republic of Cyprus and can stay on the island for up to 3 months.

In Northern Cyprus, most visitors, including citizens of the EU, USA, Canada, Australia and New Zealand, require only a valid passport. When you enter Northern Cyprus (whether from the south, Ercan airport or Kyrenia harbour), you must fill in a visa paper with your personal details and passport number. Your paper will then be stamped, and you must keep it to surrender upon exit.

Customs Regulations

Visitors from a non-EU country may bring in 200 cigarettes, one litre of spirits, four litres of wine and 250 millilitres of perfume. The import of perishable food items is strictly prohibited. Visitors may import any amount of euros or foreign banknotes, but amounts over ten thousand should be declared to customs on arrival. There are no restrictions at all in Northern Cyprus, which uses the Turkish lira (TL).

Travel Insurance

Travel insurance is advisable, and should cover theft, loss, medical problems, and any delays to travel arrangements.

Travel Safety Advice

Visitors can get up-to-date travel safety information from the Foreign and Commonwealth Office in the UK, the State Department in the US, and the Department of Foreign Affairs and Trade in Australia.

Health

Cyprus is free from most dangerous infectious diseases (although HIV is present) and no immunizations are required. Drinking tap water is safe.

EU Citizens are entitled to free or cheaper medical care in the Republic of Cyprus, provided they carry a valid European Health Insurance Card (EHIC).

You will find listings of local pharmacies in the English-language *Cyprus Mail* or by dialling 11892. These sell a full range of medicines and remedies, but if you need specialist prescription drugs it is best to bring an adequate supply with you.

All government-run General Hospitals have accident and emergency departments.

Personal Security

Cyprus is a relatively safe destination, although petty theft, such as bag snatching, does take place, particularly in the main tourist resorts. Rental cars can also be a target so ensure any valuables are locked in the boot of the car. Credit card fraud is on the increase so keep a record of all card transactions and check your bill on your return home.

Scams run by time-share touts are fairly common in the main southern Cypriot resorts, especially Pafos. Avoid any apparently "free" sightseeing tour which will inevitably result in a hard-sell presentation. Likewise, you should beware of any unsolicited offers of "help", as these are often a ploy designed to distract you.

Currency and Banking

The official currency of the Republic of Cyprus is the euro. Northern Cyprus uses the Turkish lira, though euros and pounds are readily accepted at hotels and restaurants at a decent rate.

There are 24-hour automatic teller machines in the centre of all main resorts and towns in the south. ATMs are reliable only in Kyrenia, Nicosia and Famagusta in the north.

All major credit cards are widely accepted in the Republic of Cyprus. However, fewer places in Northern Cyprus accept credit cards.

Telephone and Internet

Mobile phone usage is universal in Cyprus, and visitors who bring their own phone are likely to experience few problems. If you have an international GSM-equipped phone, check with your local service provider if global roaming is available. Alternatively, consider buying a SIM card which will cost around €20.

The country code for Cyprus is 357 except in Northern Cyprus, where it is 90 (for Turkey) then followed by (0)392 for landlines, but 533, 542 or 535 for mobiles. It is advisable not to roam with a home mobile in Northern Cyprus as the call rates are high. All numbers in the south, whether fixed or mobile,

have eight digits; subscriber numbers in the north have seven.

Wi-Fi is widespread in the south and available in the better hotels, bars and restaurants. Wi-Fi is less universal in the north, where Internet cafés remain common.

Postal Services

Letterboxes throughout the island are painted yellow. You can also post letters at the reception desk of most hotels.

The main post offices in Nicosia, Larnaka, Pafos and Limassol are open Monday to Friday 8am–5:30pm. Post offices in Northern Cyprus are open 8am–1pm and 2–5pm Monday to Friday, and 9am–noon on Saturdays.

Letters and postcards sent to European countries from the Republic of Cyprus usually arrive quickly, taking about four days. Packages sent from Northern Cyprus will take longer to reach as all mail goes via Turkey.

DIRECTORY

EMBASSIES AND CONSULATES IN THE REPUBLIC OF CYPRUS

Australian High Commission
MAP Q3 ■ Pindarou St 27, Nicosia
📞 2275 3001
🌐 cyprus.embassy.gov.au

Canadian Honorary Consulate
MAP F3 ■ Margarita House 15, Themistokli Dervi Ave, Nicosia
📞 2277 5508

Irish Embassy
MAP F3 ■ Aiantos 7, Nicosia
📞 2281 8183
🌐 dfa.ie/irish-embassy/cyprus

UK High Commission
Alexandrou Palli, Nicosia
MAP F3
📞 2286 1100
🌐 gov.uk/government/world/cyprus

US Embassy
MAP F3 ■ cnr Metohiou & Agiou Ploutarhou, Engomi
📞 2239 3939
🌐 cyprus.usembassy.gov

EMBASSIES AND CONSULATES IN NORTHERN CYPRUS

Annexe of Australian High Commission
Güner Türkmen Sokak 20, Köşklüçiflik, North Nicosia
📞 227 7332
🌐 dfat.gov.au/missions/countries/cy.html

UK High Commission
MAP F3 ■ Mehmet Akif Caddesi 29, Köşklüçiflik
📞 228 3861
🌐 gov.uk/government/world/organisations/british-high-commission-nicosia

US Embassy
MAP F3 ■ Guner Turkmen Sokak 20, Köşklüçiflik
📞 227 2443
🌐 cyprus.usembassy.gov

EMERGENCY NUMBERS IN THE REPUBLIC OF CYPRUS

Police, Ambulance, Fire: 112 or 199 Forest Fire: 1407

EMERGENCY NUMBERS IN NORTHERN CYPRUS

Police
📞 155

Ambulance
📞 112

Fire
📞 199

Forest Fire
📞 177

TRAVEL SAFETY ADVICE

Australia
Department of Foreign Affairs and Trade
🌐 dfat.gov.au
🌐 smartraveller.gov.au

UK
Foreign and Commonwealth Office
🌐 gov.uk/foreign-travel-advice

US
US Department of State
🌐 travel.state.gov

HOSPITALS

Famagusta General Hospital
📞 23 200 000

Larnaka General Hospital
📞 24 800 360

Limassol General Hospital
📞 25 801 232

Nicosia General Hospital
📞 22 603 000

Pafos General Hospital
📞 26 803 100

Polis Hospital
📞 26 821 800

Radio, TV and Newspapers

The majority of Cyprus's TV and radio stations are transmitted in Greek (in the south) and Turkish (in the north). In the Republic of Cyprus the state-run **Cyprus Broadcasting Corporation (CYBC)** has news bulletins in English at 1:30pm daily on Radio 2 (91.1FM). British Forces Broadcasting operates 24 hours a day in English on 89.7FM. BFBS 2 broadcasts on 89.9FM. In Northern Cyprus you can listen to Bayrak International which plays on 105 FM. CYBC also has news in English at 9:10pm on TV Channel 2, while most hotels offer a wider range of multilingual channels.

The Republic of Cyprus's English language newspapers are the **Cyprus Mail** (daily except Monday) and the **Cyprus Weekly** (Friday). In Northern Cyprus you'll find the *Hürriyet*. UK dailies and German and French newspapers are widely available on both sides of the border, a day after publication.

Opening Hours

Shops are open 9am–7pm on weekdays, with a long lunch break; closing at 2pm on Wednesdays, and 9am–2pm on Saturday. Banks are open 8:30am–12:30pm on weekdays in the Republic of Cyprus. In Northern Cyprus, they are open 8am–1:30pm and 2:30–6:30pm on weekdays, and 8am–noon on Saturday; big supermarkets also open on Sundays. Restaurants are usually open 11am–3pm and 7am–10:30pm daily. The hours for museums and major sights vary but tend to be 9am–5pm from Tuesday to Friday and 9am–noon on Saturday.

Time Difference

Cyprus is normally 2 hours ahead of GMT and 7 hours ahead of EST. All of Cyprus uses daylight saving time in the summer months with clocks going forward one hour on the last weekend in March and back 1 hour in the last weekend in October.

Electrical Appliances

Cyprus uses 240V/50Hz and three-pronged plugs; the same as the UK. If you're travelling from the USA or Europe, you should bring adaptors with you. Some hotels are equipped with hairdryers and irons.

Weather

Cyprus's hot summers and mild winters make it a year-round destination. Temperatures on the coast rarely fall much below 11°C (52°F), but snow often falls in the Troödos Mountains. December to February are the coolest, wettest months, while July and August the hottest, with temperatures rising well over 40°C (104°F).

The sun can be strong even on overcast days, and it is advisable to use sunscreen that is at least SPF 30. For children and those with fair or sensitive skin, an SPF of 40 or 50 is recommended. Try to avoid direct sunlight between 11am and 1pm.

Travellers with Disabilities

Sadly, few museums, archaeological sites or other attractions provide Braille or audio guides for visually impaired people, nor induction loop devices for those with hearing difficulties. Few public buildings, shops or visitor attractions have wheel-chair ramps so access can be very difficult for wheelchair users. Many museums are in older buildings without lifts, and access to archaeological sites can be difficult. Hotels, however, have plenty of ramps and lifts (the south is better than the north in this regard). Ramps at pedestrian crossings are also on the increase.

Sources of Information

The **Cyprus Tourism Organization (CTO)**, representing the Republic of Cyprus, has overseas offices in the UK, USA, Germany, Australia and elsewhere – see their website for addresses. The **North Cyprus Tourism Centre** also has overseas offices, including in the UK, Germany and Sweden.

The CTO has several outlets in southern Cyprus where you can collect maps and information on the island. There are also several unofficial websites that you may find helpful during your stay, including a growing number of blogs, such as the **Cyprus Blog**, which includes listings and general information about the Republic of Cyprus.

The **CyprusExpat** site is geared towards the expat community. The best one for events listings is **Cyprus Events**, easily searchable and regularly updated.

Trips and Tours

For city walking tours check at the relevant tourist office. The **Nicosia CTO** offers excellent twice weekly walking tours of the Old City *(see p64)* and other tourist offices, including Pafos, Limassol and Larnaka, offer similar tours. Check the relevant office for more information as well as details of other local tours. There is a hop-on-hop-off sight-seeing bus every 90 minutes which takes in the top sights in Pafos. In Larnaka, **Larnaka City Cruisers** offer guided tricycle tours of the city, lasting about an hour, departing from Plateia Evropis on the Finikoudes. In Kyrenia, Northern Cyprus, **Örnek Holidays** organizes back country safari and birding tours.

Photography

Generally, you can take photographs throughout the island without causing concern, but there are a few rules of which you should be aware.

You should not attempt to take photographs anywhere close to the "Attila Line", particularly in and around Nicosia, where sensitivities run high. There are warning signs so take heed otherwise you may find your memory chip erased. Ferry ports, airports and government installations

generally do not permit photography so it is prudent to keep your camera out of sight when exploring these locations.

Do not attempt to take photographs of aircraft or personnel at any military camp or installation on either side of the border, but particularly in Northern Cyprus where they tend to be more sensitive.

Photography without flash or tripod is some-times allowed in museums but do check the rules in advance. Churches and monas-teries with frescoes or icons do not allow flash photography but will often permit high-ISO hand-held work.

Smoking

Smoking is prohibited inside public transport, restaurants, bars and cafés in the south. Similar rules prevail in the north. It is forbidden to smoke while driving. Across the island, smokers can find smoking areas on outdoor terraces.

Tipping

In both the north and south a 10 per cent service charge is usually added to a restaurant bill. If this is not the case then a tip of a similar percentage is expected. Taxi drivers and porters generally expect a small tip; a euro will be sufficient in these cases. Bargaining is not expected in shops on either side of the border, though discounts may apply to multiple purchases.

Timeshare Touts

You may well be accosted by very pushy time-share touts at the main resorts in Cyprus, particularly in Pafos or Limassol. If you truly love the island then a time-share may be worth considering. You need to ensure that you are provided with all your rights and obligations in writing, especially where management companies promise to sell your time-share for you if you decide to exchange for another property.

The so-called free sightseeing tours, usually a quick whizz through a theme park, almost always involve having to sit through a longwinded, heavy sales pitch from commission-hungry staff, who will be pressuring you to buy. If you are definitely not interested, be sure to say no upfront. If you do decide to make a purchase, you should ascertain that there is a cooling off period when you can receive a total refund if necessary.

Toilets

Most toilets will display a sign requesting that you do not flush toilet paper due to poor plumbing throughout the island, which can cause a blockage. Wastepaper bins are provided for this purpose and it is also a prudent idea to carry a small packet of tissues and hand wipes with you when you are travelling around the island.

Shopping

For the widest choice and range of shops, head to Nicosia, where there are two main shopping areas. In the new city, Leoforos Archiepiskopou Makariou tou Tritou is home to some international chains, such as Zara (also in Pafos, Larnaka and Limassol) and Mango (also in Larnaka and Limassol). Debenhams also operates under licence in the four biggest southern cities as does Marks & Spencer. Art and crafts can be found around Laïki Geitonia in the old city. Merchants here are geared towards tourists, but still offer traditional items such as lacework and hand-carved backgammon sets at more competitive prices than the main tourist resorts. Pafos is home to the largest shopping mall in Cyprus – **Kings Avenue Mall**, while North Nicosia is the place to pick up embroidered silk, hand-painted tiles, quality rakı (cheapest in Lemar supermarkets) and inexpensive informal wear.

Dining

Cyprus has several places to eat: as well as traditional tavernas, serving Greek-and Turkish-influenced dishes, there are also French, Italian, Argentine, Chinese, Thai, Indian, Middle Eastern, Russian and even Japanese restaurants. Fish is the most expensive item and the range of fresh seafood is limited; the Karpasia (Karpaz) peninsula is the best place for it. Around the island there are stalls or bakeries selling turnovers or sandwiches as snacks.

Cyprus has very few dedicated vegetarian restaurants. Vegetable dishes may contain meat stock in both the north and the south. However, many traditional *meze* dishes, such as hummus, tahini, and grilled *halloumi* cheese are tasty and meat-free, and there are plenty of fresh fruit and salad vegetables available.

The most typical Greek Cypriot restaurant is the *mageireio* or cook-house, which you will find in larger towns and which typically serves reasonably priced, traditional dishes plus a range of drinks including wine by the carafe. There are also more upmarket tavernas, although their cuisine will generally still be based on traditional dishes, perhaps with an innovative twist.

Some establishments specialize in *meze*, and may not have an à la carte menu. In the south, all major towns and resorts are full of trendy cafés, which serve all types of Western coffee and a limited range of alcohol.

In Northern Cyprus, a *meze* taverna is known as a *meyhanes*, while a *lokanta* is a more informal dining venue. Another Anatolian import is the *pideci* or Turkish pizza parlour. Stalls or small sit-down premises in northern towns offer grilled kebabs, or *börek* as a snack which is an excellent breakfast. A 10 per cent service charge is automatically added to restaurant bills so tipping is optional.

Aside from a handful of top-end and very formal restaurants, children are welcome at restaurants and cafés, with high chairs and children's menus usually available.

Drinking

Tap water is safe to drink but not very tasty except in the Troödos Mountains. With seasonal, local fruit harvests including citrus, strawberries, peaches, bananas and guavas, fresh blended fruit juices are a delicious alternative. Squeeze is a chain of juice bars present in major towns and resorts of the south.

If you are seeking something stronger, Cyprus produces a wide range of local wines (see pp62–3). The quality, especially of the bulk wine available in jugs or carafes does vary considerably; you can ask to taste and reject it if unsatisfactory. Mediocre wine can be made palatable with soda water. The famous sweet dessert wine of Cyprus, made from sun-dried grapes in the Limassol foothills is called *commandaria*. There is just a single winery in the north, Chateau St Hilarion.

The most popular spirits, both made from grape pomace are the anise-laced ouzo and the indigenous, unflavoured *zivania* which is stronger. Cypriots also love brandy sour, which has a strange legend attached to it. The young Muslim King Farouk of Egypt habitually drank this when he was staying in Platres, in the Troödos mountains, as it looked – to others – like iced tea.

The most widespread local southern beer is KEO lager, although imported beers are also available, as well as craft beers from the sole microbrewery, Aphrodite's Rock (see p63). In the north, beer choices are restricted to the Turkish import, Efes, or a number of real ales produced by Chateau St Hilarion since 2015.

Accommodation

All hotels in the Republic of Cyprus are graded from one to five stars by the Cyprus Tourism Organization. Those in Northern Cyprus are graded in the same way, but by the North Cypriot tourism ministry. In general, it is best to avoid hotels with fewer than three stars as they are likely to be in poor locations with few facilities.

Holiday apartments in southern Cyprus are classified A, B or C by the Cyprus Tourism Organization. Most have a shared pool, a small, basic kitchen with cooker, fridge, and one to three bedrooms. Luxury apartments may have a full kitchen with dishwasher, maid and linen service.

Villas usually have a private pool, parking space, garden or patio, and a barbecue area as well as a fully equipped kitchen with a washing machine and dishwasher, up to four bedrooms, and amenities such as music systems and satellite TV.

An increasing number of stylishly restored houses and cottages can be found, mostly in the villages of the Limassol and Pafos foothills, offering character, charm and a taste of local life. Most of them have modern kitchens plus bedrooms and lounges decorated with warm traditional fabrics and antiques. Some have a small garden or terrace. Most hotels offer cheaper deals in low season (mid-November to mid-March) except for the Christmas period. Many seaside ones close early January to early March. Rates are at their highest, and rooms hardest to find, from mid-June to mid-September.

If you book a package holiday you're likely to find it is cheaper than booking hotels and flights seperately, although it offers less freedom on your holiday.

Hotels in Cyprus can be reserved from abroad via their own or a bookings website. Booking your hotel room in advance is strongly advised. Much accommodation in Cyprus is contracted out one or more years in advance by large holiday companies and finding a comfortable room on arrival may be very difficult.

Tipping is optional but welcomed in hotels in both the north and south. If someone has offered good service, a small gratuity is the norm.

DIRECTORY

SHOPPING

Kings Avenue Mall
Tombs of the Kings Ave
2, Paphos 8078
☎ 357 70 007777
w kingsavenuemall.com

Accommodation Booking Sites
w hotelscombined.com
w booking.com
w trivago.com
w expedia.com
w lastminute.com
w agoda.com

Places to Stay

PRICE CATEGORIES
For a standard, double room per night (with breakfast if included), taxes and extra charges.

....

€ under €100   €€ €100–300   €€€ over €300

Luxury Hotels

Alexander The Great Beach Hotel, Pafos
MAP A5 ▪ Poseidonos ▪ 26 965 000 ▪ www.kanikahotels.com ▪ Dis. access ▪ €€
The garden cabanas are the best feature of this beachside hotel. Both indoor and outdoor pools are the biggest around. The bar drinks are top-notch and affordable and the on-site Japanese diner, Kiku, is excellent.

Alion Beach, Ayia Napa
MAP J4 ▪ Kyro Nero Beach ▪ 23 722 900 ▪ www.alion.com ▪ €€
The best five-star hotel in town with helpful staff, a glorious beach nearby, a spa and pool. Guests can enjoy tasty breakfasts outside. Rooms are large and comfortable with minimal decor.

Ayii Anargyri Natural Healing Spa Resort, Miliou
MAP B4 ▪ Miliou outskirts ▪ 26 814 003 ▪ www.aasparesort.com ▪ Dis. access ▪ €€
Built around a natural mineral spring and incorporating the remains of a medieval monastery, this resort is open all year round and has a huge, naturally lit spa, lovely rooms and excellent food in its wine cellar restaurant.

Lokàl Hotel, Larnaca
MAP G5 ▪ Agiou Lazarou 98 ▪ 24 023 102 ▪ www.lokalcyprus.com ▪ Dis. access ▪ €€
Situated partly in a converted *belle époque* mansion, this boutique hotel is spearheading the revivial of Larnaca's old town. Attractions include a hi-tech new wing, excellent breakfasts and inviting common areas.

Palm Beach Hotel & Bungalows, Larnaka
MAP H4 ▪ Voroklini coast, Dekelia Road ▪ 24 846 600 ▪ www.palmbeachhotel.com ▪ Dis. access ▪ €€
This beachside favourite has vast gardens, plenty of parking, a water sports programme and a spa.

Anassa, Latchi
MAP A4 ▪ 26 888 000 ▪ www.anassa.com ▪ €€€
Flagship of the Thanos luxury hotels chain, the Anassa perches amid lush landscape above one of the best beaches on Cyprus. The hotel never feels full owing to its clever design. It boasts two outdoor pools, good water sports on the beach, luxurious premium suites and a stunning spa.

The Annabelle, Pafos
MAP A5 ▪ Poseidonos 10 ▪ 26 885 000 ▪ www.annabelle.com.cy ▪ Dis. access ▪ €€€
With 6 acres (2 ha) of seafront gardens, pool with a swim-up bar, this old-fashioned hotel caters to slightly older clientele who are interested in booking long winter stays.

Four Seasons, Limassol
MAP D6 ▪ Agios Tychonas ▪ 25 858 000 ▪ www.fourseasons.com.cy ▪ Dis. access ▪ €€€
Water sports off the beach, top service standards, lovely rooms, superb restaurants and other excellent facilities have long made Four Seasons one of the best hotels in Cyprus.

Grecian Park Hotel, Protaras
MAP J4 ▪ Konnos Beach ▪ 23 844 000 ▪ www.grecianpark.com ▪ Dis. access ▪ €€€
Midway between Protaras and Ayia Napa, the five-star Grecian Park is gloriously isolated but also within easy reach of both resorts. There are superb views from the comfortable sea-view suites which is the grade to go for.

Hilton Cyprus, Nicosia
MAP F3 ▪ Archiepiskopou Markariou tou Tritou 98 ▪ 22 377 777 ▪ www.hilton.com ▪ Dis. access ▪ €€€
Well located and elegant, this Hilton is the only five-star hotel in Nicosia. It provides a good mix of business and leisure facilities, including indoor and outdoor pools, helpful staff and cozy rooms.

All-Inclusive and Activity Resorts

Jubilee Hotel, Troödos

MAP C4 ▪ Troödos Square, 1504 ▪ 25 420 107 ▪ www.jubileehotel.com ▪ €

The highest hotel in Cyprus is ensconced in the pine forests of the Troödos mountains. The rooms are simple but comfortable with basic amenities. On offer are a range of activities such as skiing, hiking and cycling trails. The hotel also conducts numerous activities during the holidays for kids through its Club Jubilee.

Aktea Beach Tourist Village, Ayia Napa

MAP J4 ▪ Neofytou Poullou 10 ▪ 23 845 000 ▪ www.akteabeach.com ▪ Dis. access ▪ €€

With a beachside location, this large up-market "tourist village" accommodation has indoor and outdoor pools and a well-equipped gym.

Atlantica Miramare Beach, Limassol

MAP D6 ▪ Amerikanas, Potamos Germasogeias ▪ 25 883 500 ▪ atlanticahotels.com ▪ Dis. access ▪ €€

A state-of-the-art fitness club and spa, fully staffed by trained instructors, sets this hotel apart. There is an indoor sun-room pool for cooler days, plus tennis courts for fine days.

Louis Ledra Beach, Pafos

MAP A5 ▪ 26 964 848 ▪ louishotels.com/louis-ledra-beach.html ▪ Dis. access ▪ €€

This four-star resort has comfortable rooms and a range of all-inclusive facilities, including adults' and children's pools, a big playground, three excellent bars and a superb restaurant. A 5-minute drive from Pafos, it is on one of the area's best beaches.

Family-Friendly Resorts

Atlantica Aeneas Resort & Spa, Ayia Napa

MAP J4 ▪ Leoforos Nissi 40 ▪ 23 724 000 ▪ www.atlanticahotels.com ▪ Dis. access ▪ €€

With its huge pool, this is the epitome of family-friendly luxury, behind Ayia Napa's favourite beach. There is even a mini-club for children.

Avanti Holiday Village, Pafos

MAP A5 ▪ Poseidonos ▪ 26 965 555 ▪ www.avantihotel.com ▪ Dis. access ▪ €€

Designed with families in mind, this purpose-built village of well-equipped one-bedroom apartments has a kids' club, children's pool with a lazy river and playground, plus a separate pool, gym and sauna for adults.

The King Jason, Pafos

MAP A5 ▪ 26 947 750 ▪ www.thekingjasonpaphos.com ▪ Dis. access ▪ €€

This four-star resort complex, renovated in 2014, is divided into studios or one-bedroom apartments. There are four outdoor pools, one indoor pool. Access to the gym and sauna is free.

Louis Althea Beach, Protaras

MAP J4 ▪ 23 814 141 ▪ louishotels.com/louis-althea-beach.html ▪ Dis. access ▪ €€

Overlooking Louma Cove is this delightful apartment resort with accommodation in 150 studios or one- and two-bedrooms set in landscaped gardens. Amenities here include three eateries, a supermarket, bar, health suite and sports facilities. Children have their own kids' club, plus a pool and playground, and a varied programme of entertainment is offered.

Malama Beach Holiday Village, Paralimni

MAP J4 ▪ Above Skoutari Cave ▪ 23 822 000 ▪ www.malamaholidayvillage.com ▪ Dis. access ▪ €€

The Malama's 166 one- and two-bedroom suites all have patios or verandahs, fully equipped kitchens and satellite TV. The two-bedroom suites have two bathrooms and accommodate families of up to six. For kids, there's a grassy playground, a designated pool, tennis, and the Malamino Kids Club offering parties, mini-discos, beach games and excursions.

Olympic Lagoon Resort, Ayia Napa

MAP J4 ▪ 23 722 500 ▪ kanikahotels.com ▪ Dis. access ▪ €€

This resort has seven swimming pools, five all-inclusive eateries and a spa. For kids, there are clubs by age group and a football academy. It is a popular venue for wedding parties.

Almyra, Pafos
MAP A5 ▪ Poseidonos
12 ▪ 26 888 700 ▪ www.
almyra.com ▪ €€€
The Almyra is a family-
friendly design-led hotel,
co-managed with The
Annabelle. There is a
separate children's pool
with a sun canopy and a
kids' club operating from
Easter to October and
during Christmas week.
It also hosts triathlon
athletes during the winter
training season. On-site
bicycle hire.

Columbia Beachotel, Pissouri
MAP C6 ▪ 25 833 333
▪ www.columbiabeach.
com ▪ Dis. access ▪ €€€
Well-established
four-star hotel where
the larger suites can
accommodate families
of up to four people.
Rates are all-inclusive
and children's menus are
provided. It is just uphill
from the larger resort
hotel under the same
management *(see p128)*.

Suites and Apartments

Eleonora, Larnaka
MAP G5 ▪ Ermou 55
▪ 24 624 400 ▪ www.eleo
norahotelapts.com ▪ €
Centrally located, the
Eleanora offers spacious,
light-filled studios and
two-room suites complete
with proper kitchens and
contemporary bathrooms.

Stephanos Hotel Apartments, Polis
MAP A4 ▪ Arsinois 8
▪ 26 322 411 ▪ www.
stephanos-hotel.com
▪ Dis. access ▪ €
The two wings flank
a large central pool.
A mix of studio and
one-bedroom apartments
are well maintained
and have excellent
facilities, including
well-equipped kitchens
with ovens. There are
private balconies and
the downstairs restaurant
serves good Cypriot food.

Tavros Apartments, Polis
MAP A4 ▪ Neo Chorio
Village ▪ 26 322 421
▪ www.tavroshotel.
com ▪ €
Neo Chorio is the gateway
village to the Akamas
wilderness and this is the
best base there.Choose
one of the six studios or
24 one-bedroom apart-
ments, where kitchens
are basic but bathrooms
are quite modern.

Corallia Beach, Pafos
MAP A5 ▪ Coral Bay
▪ 26 622 121 ▪ corallia
beachhotel.com ▪ €€
Overlooking Coral Bay,
this complex of studios
and one-bedroom
apartments has a fine
location and a good range
of facilities, including
a restaurant, bar, pool
plus a gym and a sauna.

Napa Mermaid, Ayia Napa
MAP J4 ▪ Kryou Nerou 45
▪ 23 721 606 ▪ napa
mermaidhotel.com ▪ €€
The USP of this reinvented
designer hotel are the
junior suites, with big
balconies and plush
furnishings. The grand
suites are essentially two-
bedroom apartments,
with a Jacuzzi outside on
the terrace. Pool, tennis
court, two full-service
restaurants and an
Elemis spa on-site. Pro-
active staff and plenty of
free goodies.

Columbia Beach Resort, Pissouri
MAP C6 ▪ 25 833 000
▪ www.columbiaresort.
com ▪ Dis. access ▪ €€€
The 95 luxury suites, right
above Pissouri beach are
all roofed with recycled
earthenware tiles in the
style of a traditional village.
There is no kitchen, so
the rate includes a buffet
breakfast. Smaller suites
can be connected as
family accommodation.
The spa is stunning.

Villas

Bougainvillea, Polis
MAP A4 ▪ West of Polis
▪ 26 812 250 ▪ www.
bougainvillea.com.cy ▪ €€
Choose between two
villas here, each sleeping
six people and each with
its own pool, between
unpretentious Polis and
hideaway Neo Chorio. The
beaches of Chrysochou
Bay, the harbour tavernas
of Lakki and the forested
wilderness of the Akamas
peninsula are not far away.

Chrysanthia, Neo Chorio
MAP A4 ▪ Neo Chorio
8852 ▪ www.villa
chrysanthia.com ▪ €€
A larger-than-average
family villa of over three
storeys – it can sleep
up to eight people in air-
conditioned comfort, with
its own small pool and
off-road parking. It is also
close to Asprokremmos
beach and Latchi port.

The Olympians Latchi Beach Villas, Polis
MAP A4 ▪ 99 773 647
▪ www.the-olympians.
com ▪ €€
Complex of 10 two- and
three- bedroom seaside
villas can accommodate

four to six people. The two-storey houses are very well-appointed, set around plantings of palm trees and flowering oleander. Each villa has good Wi-Fi and also benefits from its own pool and views of the sea.

Royal Garden Villas, Pafos

MAP A5 ▪ Vassilis Verenikis St ▪ 26 844 444 ▪ Dis. access ▪ €€€
Each of the Elysium's 12 Royal Villas has its own landscaped garden and private pool. Although linked to the Elysium Hotel, they can only be booked through specialist agencies such as Classic Collection.

Rural Hotels and Agrotourism

Cyprus Villages

MAP E5 ▪ Tochni ▪ 24 332 998 ▪ www.cyprus villages.com.cy ▪ €
Lodging is at the restored buldings in Tochni, Kalavasos and Psematis-menos villages, as well as modern centrally heated apartments in Tochni (suitable for winters). Car rental from Pafos or Larnaka airports is included in package. Horse riding and mountain biking are also available.

Lasa Heights, Pafos

MAP B4 ▪ Archiepiskopou Makariou 91 ▪ 26 732 777 ▪ www.lasaheights.com ▪ Dis. access ▪ €
Partly occupying what used to be a 19th-century village *kafeneio*, this nine-room inn has very helpful proprietors and is perhaps the quietest hotel in the area, with sweeping

views from Pafos to Polis. Other rooms are in the newly built wing with modern decor.

Lofou Agrovino, Lofou

MAP C5 ▪ 25 470 202 ▪ www.agrovinolofou. com ▪ €
This range of restored cottages, open all year round, combines trad-itional and practical decor and offers good Wi-Fi as well. Breakfast is included – served either in the affiliated restaurant or their wine bar.

Paradiso Hills, Lyso

MAP B4 ▪ Lysos village, Polis ▪ 26 322 287 ▪ www. paradisoshills.com ▪ €
This stone-clad, hilltop hotel caters to weddings and also has fabulous views, excellent food and top-notch decor.

Rodon Hotel, Agros

MAP D4 ▪ Rodou 1, 4860 ▪ 25 521 201 ▪ www.rodonhotel.com ▪ Dis. access ▪ €
Named after the Greek word for scented rose, the Rodon has sumptuous rooms, stylish lounge areas and an on-site restaurant that serves excellent traditional food. Take in the panoramic views and the rustic charm of the Agros village while enjoying all modern amenities. Free Wi-Fi access.

To Spitikou tou Arhonta, Treis Elies

MAP C4 ▪ 99 527 117 ▪ www.spitiko3elies. com ▪ €
Located above the village, this charmingly rustic accommodation offers one-, and two-bedroom

apartments, which are fully equipped and set in a pretty, shady garden. Traditional meals including breakfast are available on request.

Vasilopoulos House, Tochni

MAP E5 ▪ 24 332 531 ▪ www.vasilopoulos house.com.cy ▪ €
One of the oldest houses in Tochni now contains three one-bedroom apartments and four studios, each with its own kitchen and all opening onto a shady courtyard.

Casale Panayiotis, Kalopanagiotis

MAP C4 ▪ 22 952 444 ▪ www.casalepanayiotis. com ▪ €€
Studio units are dispersed among stone houses in the old quarter of this Troödos village. Most of them have working fireplaces or wood-stoves. The place operates many eateries such as the Byzantine full-service restaurant and a break-fast salon. It also has the stunning Myrianthousa spa, an outdoor pool and adjacent gym; all have valley views. Free Wi-Fi throughout.

Kontoyannis House, Kalavasos

MAP E5 ▪ 25 584 131 ▪ www.kontoyiannis.com ▪ €€
This old village home in the centre of Kalavasos has been tastefully con-verted into three studios and apartments, sharing a pretty courtyard, plus a five-bedroom family villa nearby. There is free Wi-Fi throughout and a small wellness centre.

The Library, Kalavasos
MAP E5 ■ 24 817 071 ■ www.libraryhotel cyprus.com ■ €€
Formerly a 19th-century *kervansaray* (roadside inn), this hotel and wellness retreat has a library with books in five languages. Breakfast is served in the central courtyard, dinner in the Mitos Restaurant. Rooms have Jacuzzi tubs and underfloor heating.

Linos Inn, Kakopetria
MAP D4 ■ 22 923 161 ■ www.linosinn.com ■ €€
Thirty-four interlinked 19th-century dwellings make this a romantic and quirky inn. River-view studios have terraces, Jacuzzis and fireplaces while executive suites have a kitchen.

Stratos ArtDeco House, Kalavasos
MAP E5 ■ 24 332 293 ■ www.stratos-house. cyprushotel.net ■ €€
Stratos is only steps away from the village square, with a beautiful arcaded courtyard off which open two large studio rooms, each with its own en-suite and kitchenette. On the upper floor is a lovely vine-covered verandah. Sensitively renovated, this house retains a great deal of its original character.

Northern Cyprus Resorts

Almond Holiday Village, Kyrenia
MAP F2 ■ Bademli Sokak, Alsancak (Karavas) ■ 0392 821 28 85 ■ www. almond-holidays.com ■ €€
Surrounded by forest and set in gardens of lawns

and exotic flowers, this relaxed holiday village offers a choice of accommodation in garden bungalows, galleried villas and standard doubles. Facilities include an attractive pool and sun terrace area, a welcoming lounge bar and a restaurant. Friendly staff provide excellent service.

Denizkızı Royal Hotel, Kyrenia
MAP F2 ■ Dumlupınar Sokak Alsancak (Karavas) ■ 0392 821 26 76 ■ info@ denizkizi.com ■ €€
Wooded grounds surround the suites here, which have Jacuzzis and unimpeded sea views. There is an array of bars and restaurants, a huge swimming pool, fitness centre and a choice of water sports down on the sandy cove.

Merit Crystal Cove Hotel, Kyrenia
MAP F2 ■ 0392 821 23 45 ■ www.merithotels.com ■ Dis. access ■ €€
Perched above the sea about 15 km (10 miles) west of Kyrenia, this huge modern hotel would not look out of place in Las Vegas. With landscaped grounds, two swimming pools, a private beach and one of Northern Cyprus's smartest casinos, it really feels like a tropical island celebrity hideaway.

Oscar Resort Hotel, Kyrenia
MAP F2 ■ 0392 815 48 01 ■ www.oscar-resort.com ■ €€
The Oscar Resort Hotel offers spacious rooms and suites, a spa, reliable on-site car rental and decent food. There are three outdoor pools which

is handy since the nearby Karakum beach is not the best for a swim.

Pia Bella, Kyrenia
MAP F2 ■ Iskenderun Caddesi 14 ■ 0392 815 53 21 ■ www.piabella. com ■ €€
Close to the harbour, this lavishly landscaped hotel complex has two pools, one of them is 25-m (82-ft) long. The double suites in the rear wings are preferable to the main building.

Salamis Bay Conti Resort
MAP J3 ■ 0392 378 82 00 ■ info@salamisbayconti. com ■ Dis. access ■ €€
At this huge hotel most rooms have sea views. There is a spa, fitness centre and an excellent beach at the back. Avoid an out-of-season stay.

Yazade House, Kyrenia
MAP F2 ■ Yazıcızade Sokak ■ 0392 815 57 69 ■ www. theyazadehouse.com ■ €€
Owned by an English couple, this delightful trio of a summer studio, a two-person and a four-person apartment is a peaceful oasis in the old Turkish quarter of Kyrenia and has a one week minimum booking period. There is a pool in the courtyard.

Northern Cyprus Hotels

Betül Guesthouse, Famagusta
MAP J4 ■ Kuruçeşme Sok 12 ■ 0392 366 33 00 ■ www.betulkonukevi. com ■ €
A salubrious, family-friendly guesthouse in medieval Famagusta,

Betül Guesthouse has five simple and elegant en-suite rooms with good breakfasts. Other meals are provided by arrangement.

Manolya Hotel, Lapithos (Lapta)
MAP E2 ▪ 0392 821 84 98 ▪ www.manolyahotel.com ▪ Dis. access ▪ €
Located 10 km (4 miles) from Kyrenia, this modern beachside hotel makes a good budget option. There are indoor and outdoor restaurants and on-site scuba school. Rooms are well-presented and many overlook the large lagoon-style pool.

Nitovikla Garden Hotel, Karpasia Peninsula
MAP K2 ▪ Kumyalı (Koma tou Gialou) ▪ 0392 375 59 80 ▪ www.nitovikla.com ▪ €
There are 10 traditionally decorated rooms here with rustic styled furniture and colourful textiles. A lovely garden with a vegetable patch is out front. There are bicycles to rent, and an excellent restaurant.

Villa Lembos, Karpasia
MAP L1 ▪ Ayfilon Road, Dipkarpaz (Rizokarpaso) ▪ 0392 372 20 27 ▪ www.villalembos.com ▪ €
A farmstay B&B in an idyllic setting with cattle lowing, marsh frogs peeping and the proprietor rototilling his vegetable patch nearby. The 11 scattered villas have contemporary and comfortable bathrooms, beds and fridges but no kitchen. Breakfast is served in the restaurant, which also provides dinner in season. Order the lamb as it is raised on the farm.

Balcı Plaza, Karpasia Peninsula
MAP K1 ▪ 0533 824 00 44 ▪ www.balciplaza.com ▪ €€
Excellent small hotel with its own beach and sea views from the upstairs rooms. Excellent value, friendly management and a good restaurant to return to in the evenings make this a good touring base for the Karpasia Peninsula.

Bellapais Gardens, Bellapais
MAP F3 ▪ Crusader Rd ▪ 0392 815 60 66 ▪ www.bellapaisgardens.com ▪ €€
Close to the spectacular ruin of Bellapais Abbey, this atmospheric small chalet-hotel has fantastic views. It also has pretty gardens shaded by cypresses and palm trees, a good spring-fed pool and a well-deserved reputation for excellent Cypriot-European fusion cooking. High above sea level, it also offers a cool refuge from the blazing summer heat.

Golden Tulip, North Nicosia
MAP F3 ▪ Dereboyu Street ▪ 0392 610 5050 ▪ www.goldentulipnicosia.com ▪ €€
This business-style hotel offers slick modern rooms and excellent facilities, including a spa and Jacuzzi. Dereboyu is the main shopping, dining and entertainment boulevard of modern north Nicosia.

The Hideaway Club, Kyrenia
MAP F2 ▪ Edremit (Trimithi) ▪ 0542 845 07 71 ▪ www.hideawayclub.com ▪ €€
A poolside bar and restaurant is the heart of the club. All rooms have complimentary bathrobes, iron bed-steads, throw rugs and hammocks which you usually see only in posh hotels. Helpful and efficient staff.

Kyrenia Palace Boutique Hotel, Kyrenia
MAP F2 ▪ Cafer Pasa Sok 3 ▪ 0392 815 60 08 ▪ www.kyreniaboutiquehotel.com ▪ €€
Ideal for off-season breaks, this worthy hotel in Old Kyrenia has 11 rooms and suites with high ceilings, antique furnishings and balconies. There is also a restaurant and a small spa on the premises. Breakfast is served in a secluded courtyard.

Onar Village, Kyrenia
MAP F2 ▪ 0392 815 58 50 ▪ www.onarvillage.com ▪ €€
This underrated three-star hillside complex has great views from its 44 rooms and 20 big quiet villas. The villas are close to the pool and have individual water heaters and full kitchens, ideal for long winter breaks. The hotel wing has an ornate *hamam*, massage rooms, a sauna and an indoor pool. Shuttles to town and rental cars are available.

For a key to hotel price categories see p126

General Index